Onward Christian Soldier

E L C Slarks

Onward Christian Soldiers marching into war with the cross of Jesus going on before.........

A 19th century hymn written by Sabine Baring-Gould

On August 14th 1941, at a time when the success of the Second World War was far from certain, U.S. President Franklin D. Roosevelt and British Prime Minister Winston Churchill met on board HMS Prince of Wales to agree the Atlantic Charter. This comprised a joint declaration between Britain and the United States setting out a vision for the post war world. At a church service following the meeting, Churchill chose this hymn. Below is an extract from a radio broadcast by Churchill following the service.

"We sang Onward Christian Soldiers indeed, and I felt that this was no vain presumption, but that we had the right to feel that we were serving a cause for the sake of which a trumpet has sounded from on high. When I looked upon that densely packed congregation of fighting men of the same language, of the same faith, of the same fundamental laws, of the same ideals ... it swept across me that here was the only hope, but also the sure hope, of saving the world from measureless degradation."

First Edition, Published 2020

Acknowledgements

I acknowledge with grateful thanks the following people without whom this book could not have been produced:

- My son David who has spent many hours deciphering my writing, editing and preparing this book for publication
- My son-in-law Keith and grandson Philip for proofreading and making helpful comments
- The Historical Research Group of Sittingbourne (HRGS), Don and Jacky Harris, John Weeks and Janet Halligan for proofreading this publication and in particular Richard and Theresa Emmett who supported this publication and gave much helpful guidance and advice
- Swale Borough Council for printing this book

I apologise for any errors or inaccuracies relating to the World War 2 Normandy campaign, which are entirely my own. I give credit to the authors of my regimental history 'The Story of the 23rd Hussars', on which I have depended to help me recall unfolding events in 1944 - 45.

E L C Slarks

I dedicate this book to my five grandchildren, Rebecca, Robert, Rachel, Philip and Helen, and my six great grandchildren, Anna, Eva, Lyra, Aaron, Maya and Darcie, and to all the friends who have played a part, large or small in my long life.

Onward Christian Soldier

Contents:

Introduction

Initially Dad set out to write this book purely for his own pleasure as writing is something he enjoys. Later, when inquisitive grandchildren began to ask questions about his life, his writing gained added impetus, and he hoped that writing his story would be the best way to answer their questions. Dad wrote this book entirely in handwritten manuscript. The writing of a book extending almost 200 pages and approaching 50,000 words is no mean task. To do so in handwritten manuscript with very few amendments is particularly impressive in these days of the word processor.

This book draws significant content from Dad's autobiography 'One Step at a Time' prepared and printed purely for his family in 2003, with only a few copies being produced, and not published. However, as one of very few surviving veterans from World War 2, his story seemed to gain a broader interest over recent years, and so in his 97th year I have helped him prepare this story for a wider audience to enjoy.

Born in 1923, he has lived through one of the most turbulent periods of recent British history. The Britain of the early 21st century in which he lives now, seems a different universe to his early years in rural Kent in the 1920s and 30s. At the onset of World War 2, at the age of 19, like millions of others, he was called up to serve in the army. His life was taken over by world events for the next four years, but he was fortunate to come through and build a new life for his family in the peaceful decades that followed.

The Methodist Church has been a central thread running through his life. He has devoted over sixty years to serving as a lay preacher and his faith has been a source of inner strength which has seen him through both difficult and joyful times.

It has been a pleasure to help with the publication of this book and I hope it is of interest to those who find time to read it. As I write Dad is quarantined at home alone, to protect him from the current world war - against the Coronavirus Covid-19.

David Slarks
March 2020

Chapter 1
Childhood

I was born in the small North East Kent town of Milton Regis, on the 26th of March 1923. It is a town whose boundaries straddle those of the larger town of Sittingbourne.

Milton Regis has a long and interesting past and when I was quite young, the town had its own District Council whose un-elected but generally recognised 'Mayor' was Douglas Knowles. It was a town we were proud of and many were dismayed when its name no longer featured on the railway platform signs. It became swallowed up by Sittingbourne, which is situated on the important A2 road linking London with Canterbury.

We can trace the history of Milton Regis back to the reign of King Ethelbert I, who held the Throne of Kent between 589 - 616. It was during Ethelbert's reign that St Augustine landed somewhere near Ebbsfleet, inland from Pegwell Bay, on the Isle of Thanet, around the year 597. St Augustine made his way to the Kings Court at Canterbury bringing the Christian gospel to this country. Ethelbert was one of the first converts to this new religion.

It appears that Milton Regis was a royal estate as far back as this period. Later the Doomsday Book, dated 1086, shows the way in which Kent was divided, for administration, judicial and taxation purposes, into seven large divisions called 'lathes'. These in turn were divided into smaller areas known as 'hundreds'. Lathes are peculiar to Kent and each of them was based on an important settlement or town, which at some time had probably been a royal township. The half lathe of Milton centred on the great royal estate known as Milton Regis. The town was plundered and burnt down before the Norman Conquest by Earl Godwin in 1052 and the enormous estate of Milton Regis passed eventually to King William the Conqueror. But enough of the history of Milton Regis, what of my family background?

I was the second in a family of three, having a brother two years younger than me and a sister six years older.

My parents were poor by the standards of those days. My father was a farm labourer on a local fruit growing farm and my mother was a hardworking housewife. It was hard for them, as it was for many parents of the 1920's, bringing up a family, even as small as ours. Many had large families of ten or more and looking back I wonder how they managed to bring them up and provide for them, as well as they did. Mum often had to supplement Dad's meagre income of 30 shillings a week by doing summer seasonal work in the fields to make ends meet. The annual hop picking season, a long past feature of Kent life, provided a means of earning money, to rig us children out with clothes, when later we returned to school. It was also a kind of 'holiday' for us, for when we were not picking hops, we boys would play in the woods making bows and arrows. The season usually ended with the lighting of bonfires. Faggots, i.e. bundles of sticks, were also used during the hop picking season to make fires on which we placed 'billycans' to make tea.

Pickers were driven to the hop gardens, sometimes in steam powered lorries and later in buses. It was the early days of the motor car; anyone who had a car was considered well off.

It was, as I have said, a hard life for folk like us, but in spite of all the hardship we were a happy family. Our needs were few, just the essentials of life such as good food, adequate clothing and enough money to pay the rent.

The car had not become the essential means of transport it is today, and radio was in its infancy. There were still a few 'crystal sets' as they were called, but radio had not reached the peak of perfection that we now enjoy. Stereo sound had not been developed, though you may have been the proud owner of a gramophone, a record player usually combined with a 'wireless', as radios used to be called. Television was still a dream, as yet unfulfilled.

Our pleasures in those days were the simple ones, such as long country walks with all the family, or visiting friends, games of hopscotch and the trailing of hoops along quiet country lanes. I had a steel hoop and I travelled many a mile with it. It was also the age of the yo-yo and the skipping rope (for girls of course). Other 'treats' were the family visits to aunts and uncles in Teynham and far flung Faversham (five miles away), and Sunday School parties and outings to Sheerness in the summer. More adventurous holidays were rare. I do recall one such holiday though, under canvas at Smith's holiday camp at Leysdown with my mother's parents. My brother and I were taken in turn for a week by the sands in this outpost of The Isle of Sheppey. I can still smell the paraffin from the burning Tilley lamps we used to light our tent. I could not have been more than five or six years old.

As I grew older, another pleasure was the cinema, to which everyone flocked at least once a week. There was one in Leysdown on the Isle of Sheppey which showed silent films. I often went to the Plaza Cinema in East Street in Sittingbourne, long since demolished and replaced by a residential home for old people. My favourite films were the Janet Gaynor / Charles Farrell romantic series, and later on the films of Deanna Durbin. I think I fell in love with Deanna Durbin because she played the typical 'girl next door'. She had a natural innocent charm and also a beautiful voice. I discovered that music, well played or sung had an emotional effect on me.

**On holiday (aged 5) at Smith's Holiday Camp, Leysdown,
with Auntie and Grandmother**

I saw what I believe was the first sound picture to be shown locally
called 'Hells Angels'. This was a film about the Flying Corps,
which was the forerunner of the Royal Air Force. It was the golden
age of the cinema, and between 1930 and 1940 modern cinema
theatres seating up to 2,000 people were built. Every town of any
size had its 'picture house' to which thousands of people flocked
every day of the week.

On a site in the centre of Sittingbourne, just a mile from my home
town of Milton, the Odeon Theatre was built. It was erected
directly over the River Bourne, from which the town gets its name.
I have heard it said that pilgrims on their way to Canterbury rested
here on their journey hence the name 'Sittingbourne', though I am
not sure if this is true. The builders of the new Odeon cinema had
great difficulties laying the foundations. Piles had to be driven into
the river to form a good foundation.

Out for a country walk with sister Gladys (third from right) and brother Bert (cap in hand). I am in the middle, about 12 years old

Old men standing by would mutter, 'They'll never put up such a building there'. However, after initial problems the new theatre was completed in 1940. It was Art Deco, the predominant decorative style of the 1920 and 30s, characterised by precise and bold geometric shapes and colours. The auditorium and proscenium[1] area were luxurious. It was planned to include an organ but this was not possible. I well remember the first film shown at the new Odeon cinema. It was called 'Little Lord Fauntleroy' and starred a young actor, Freddie Bartholomew.

A visit to the cinema was the highlight of our week. To sit in the balcony, the dearer seats, and to watch the changing colours of the curtains before the film, was a real luxury for me. I was transported from the soot-ridden streets of Milton, with the constant outfall from the chimneys of the nearby paper mill, to distant places.

---

[1] The proscenium of a theatre stage is a structure in front of the stage that frames the action of the play.

'Boars' the Chemist on the corner of Bridge Street, Milton, provided a free service to those who were unfortunate enough to get specs of soot in their eyes from the paper mill nearby. Anyone who wanted to make some kind of token payment was requested to put a small donation in a tin on the counter. This money would be used to maintain the local Memorial Hospital, which had been built through the auspices of Edward Lloyd, who owned the paper mill. This hospital was modernised and extended in 1998. Mr Lloyd would have been proud to know about this.

We lived in a small terraced house in the High Street, a street which began at the head of an inlet creek of the Swale. In those early days the town centred on the creek, which was then navigable. It afforded an important means of transport for the local brick making, cement mills and paper making industries. Supplies of china clay were brought in from as far away as Cornwall for the production of newsprint. This very important waterway, known as Milton Creek twisted its way to Sittingbourne where it eventually found its way north to the Swale. Barge building was also an important trade along its banks, for it was by these craft that necessary supplies were carried. The sight of the tall red/brown sails moving slowly along the creek was a familiar one. The upper part of this waterway near the town has long since become silted up.

Being always very interested in maps, I once walked the path of the creek to its beginning at Ridham Dock and plotted its course. My drawing was not quite correct when compared to an Ordnance Survey map but it was an experience of discovery to me in those school days.

To return to my home at No 41 High Street, it was quite small. There was a sitting room on the ground floor, which was about ten inches below the level of the pavement. On entering the front door, you stepped down immediately into the room. Just inside the front door, built into the corner of the room was a cupboard. We used this to keep our toys, such as they were. We did not have much furniture, just a large table and four chairs and a long horsehair sofa, which stood against one wall. Over the fireplace was a mantle shelf around which hung a frieze. One morning a spark from the fire caught this alight. I can still remember my mother frantically tearing it down and stamping on it to put out the flames. Such floor coverings as we had, were rugs made of strips of odd bits of coloured cloth. These had been sewn painstakingly together by my mother.

A winding staircase led up to two bedrooms, a large one at the front and a smaller one at the rear of the house, set into the roof. This was the room my brother and I shared. We used to get up to all kinds of crazy pranks. One of our favourite adventures was to climb out of the bedroom window on to the sloping roof. Armed with an umbrella as a parachute we would float down to the brick paved yard below. I say float; we more or less fell, luckily never really hurting ourselves. Dad eventually found out about our little stunt and put a stop to it in no uncertain manner. Another flight of stairs led up to a garret (room in the loft) at the front of the house. This room we used for dressing up and as a playroom, putting on concerts with our friends. My father also used to store fruit here, obtained from the farm at Bobbing, a mile away where he worked. We always had plenty of fruit and vegetables to eat. The farmer was quite generous to his workmen and allowed them to take home a limited amount of produce for their own use. Behind the living room was a small kitchen. It sported a black 'Zebo' polished kitchen range and a deep stone sink ('Zebo' was the trade name for the black polish Mum used for cleaning the stove and ovens).
There was also a brick 'copper'[2] in the corner, which was used to heat water for washing our clothes. This same copper was also used for boiling the water for our Friday night baths. At Christmas it

---

[2] A copper was often built into the corner of a kitchen and comprised a large cylindrical iron tank surrounded by brickwork and heated from beneath by a coal fire.

was also filled with water, and heated to cook Christmas puddings wrapped in linen cloth.

Thinking of Christmas, an annual incident at the public house at the bottom of the high street where I lived as a child (known as Milton Hill) comes to mind. The landlord would turn out the men who had spent the morning drinking, getting home late to have their cold Christmas dinner, to an angry wife who had been looking after the children all morning. On the way home the men used to throw all their spare change into the road for the children to scramble for. We didn't have a lot of money in those days and it was something the men liked to do.

Friday night was bath night. Few homes had bathrooms in those days and it was not until I married and moved to a new house in the village of Newington, three miles away that my wife Jean and I experienced the luxury of hot running water. We had to use a long galvanised bath which usually hung outside on the wall and fill it up from the copper. Our clothes were washed in the copper on Mondays, the water being heated by a coal fire beneath it.

In the 1930s we did not have electric light or even gaslight. We used oil lamps to light the 'parlour', as the living room was called, and candles to find our way upstairs to bed. Gaslight came later and was for us a great improvement.

On Saturdays, mum would bake cakes in the little kitchen for Sunday tea. Also, to the delight of us children she would make home-made sweets, toffee, coconut ice etc. It was lovely on a cold morning, to come in from play to the smell of cooking. My mother always seemed to be busy with some necessary chores.

At the back of the house, from the kitchen, steps led up from a small yard to a garden, and at the end of it was the WC, a small brick building with a door which did not reach the floor by six inches. It was draughty with none of the comforts of the modern toilet we have today. We had to face visiting this little room in all weathers to attend to our private needs. Behind this, a wall separated the garden from the local fire station situated in Crown Road. On the other side of this wall, rockets were set off in the event of a fire to call out the crew wherever they might be. One rocket meant it was a local fire and two rockets warned of a fire in adjoining Sittingbourne. It was not unusual for a rocket to be set off when the 'little house' was occupied. The sound could be quite upsetting and give you a shock when seated 'on the throne' so to speak.

I mentioned the gramophone. Ours was one of those that had a large horn to amplify the sound. We played small six-inch shellac, (pre vinyl) records at 78 revs per minute. One of these I remember was an old recording of part of Rossini's overture to William Tell. This was, I remember, my very first experience of classical music. Whenever I play a recording of that piece on modern hi-fi equipment, my mind goes back to the thrill I first felt of hearing Rossini.

My mother loved music and, being a devoted member of Milton Salvation Army, she was also a songster in the local corps in Kingsmill Road.

I suppose it was from my mother that I got my love of music. My parents were members of the Co-operative Society, who did much to foster interest in music education in the 1920s and 30s, as well as being large grocers etc. We used to go to a hall over what is now a plumbing store in East Street, Sittingbourne. Here the Co-op organised recitals which I remember attending where artists sang old ballads such as 'Trees' and 'Old Man River' etc.

My mother, before her illness, aged about 39

Other simple pleasures, in addition to long walks in the country, were games at Milton Recreation Ground and visits to aunts and my grandparents. We walked everywhere it seemed. Sometimes the aunts would visit us at home and always wanted to kiss us boys. I hated this and hid in a toy cupboard by the front door of our house when I knew they were coming.

I was a very shy child. I imagine that I was not particularly strong either because I had to take cod liver oil and malt to build me up. I got to like it in the end. Medicines such as Syrup of Figs and sulphur, blown into our throat when it became sore, were typical of those days. As a child of five I remember travelling to Maidstone by charabanc, i.e. double-decker open top bus, to have my tonsils out. The nurse gave me a lozenge to suck before the operation and when I woke up afterwards, I found myself in a long bed covered by a red blanket. The anaesthetic had not completely worn off and my mother told me later that our bus broke down on Detling Hill on the way home and another was sent for to get us home.

We had some very kind neighbours in those days. The Rossiters, on one side, were an old couple. They loved to bet on the horses and always seemed to have an eye for the winner. On the other side, up the High Street, lived Mrs Pritchard with her daughter Nora Wise. Mrs Pritchard and her daughter were both widows. Nora lost her husband while he was working as a lighterman on the creek. He drowned in an unfortunate accident. They had never had children of their own. One day when I was quite small, she asked my mother if she could adopt me. She knew what a struggle Mum had to bring us up and she so wanted a child of her own. Of course, Mum would not hear of it but Nora took a particular interest in me. In later years she remarried to an army officer from Gillingham. They eventually adopted two boys. I well remember visiting them one weekend and attending an army parade at Brompton Barracks.

Nora's husband, Mr. Bilcliff was a very disciplined military man, very smart and strict with his two adopted sons. He made the boys clock in and out when they left the house, but they were good parents.

My dad's mother lived in a little house in Shakespeare Road in Sittingbourne, which is still there very much as it was when I was a boy. We often visited her and referred to her as 'little Gran'. She was a small lady compared to my mother's mother, Gran Taylor. Years before, I can remember Dad had a sister who married an American and went to live in California. When I was about 13 or 14 Aunt Edie came home for a holiday and stayed at Shakespeare Road. I remember she had a large trunk, in which she brought all her travelling things. She had come by sea by way of the Panama Canal. In those days it must have taken a long time to travel from

San Jacinto, where she lived. Her husband and sons ran a dairy farm with over 500 head of cattle called Big Pines Dairy. I remember her writing to us, after she went back home, on paper embossed in green with three pine trees. The town of San Jacinto I discovered was situated between a Native American reserve and the up and coming film centre of Hollywood. We found it exciting to learn we had American relatives. Aunt Edie was a little wizened faced lady with a distinct broad cowboy accent like a character out of the musical Oklahoma.

One day when we went to see Aunt Edie, she gave my brother Bert and me a large box of 'candies' as she called them. It was a box of milk chocolates. We had never had sweets such as these, although Dad would sometimes buy us toffees or boiled sweets. Aunt Edie wanted very much to take me back to America with her, me being the older one, but of course Dad would not agree with it. I often wonder now if I might have ended up as a cowboy on a ranch like the ones I had seen in Wild West films.

School

I did not take too warmly to school at first and being shy did not make friends easily. On the way I often called into a stationer's shop run by a Mr Hinge. He would appear out of the darkness to serve us with blotting paper which we used at school in those days. We used ink - biros had not been invented as far as I can remember. We often blotted our exercise books and we needed to dry the ink. We also passed the old Court Hall where it is said prisoners were kept in the old days. This hall was built in about 1450 as the judicial and administrative centre of Milton Hundreds. Here the manorial rents were collected and two high constables were appointed annually. There is an iron grill in the door through which prisoners were fed by their friends and relatives. We used to look though this grill expecting to see some unfortunate victim who had been incarcerated for getting into debt. Our imagination knew no bounds. The stocks and pillory and perhaps gallows stood close by in what is known as 'The Cross'. Since 1972 the Court Hall has been opened as a museum.

Another diversion was the forge, open to the street, where quite unaware that we might be late for school, we lingered too long. I found it fascinating to watch the smithy working the bellows of the furnace seeing the sparks fly as he did so. From the heat he would beat the horseshoes into shape and then, with the smell of burning in our nostrils, he fitted them expertly to the animal's feet. How big those horses were to us small boys. Then we would realise we must hurry on or we would be late for school and incur the wrath of Joe Coupland the headmaster. He was a very strict head but at heart a kind and understanding man. I think of the other teachers who tried to teach the essential things we needed to go out into the world. How they must have despaired of us.

I shared a desk with a boy named Brian who was always fooling about. One day, as he passed the teacher's desk, he popped a fizzing pastel into the ink well. The poor man returned to find the ink overflowing his desk and running down the sides.

Another teacher, Bert Thurlow, could not forget he once served in the Middle East in the 1st World War. During lessons he would suddenly grab the long pole which was used to open the windows and do a bayonet charge across the classroom. 'When I was in Mesopotamia' he would say, 'we had to defend ourselves in this way'. One day Joe Coupland came through the door just as he was about to perform his customary charge. Bert hastily returned the pole to its place against the wall. He used to go red in the face when boys did not concentrate on the lessons. Brian, who sat next to me always cracked jokes when we were meant to be listening. He could keep a straight and innocent face but I could not, and I often got the blame for not paying attention. When a boy really annoyed him, he would rush up the gangway between the desks, his face crimson with rage. When he reached the offending pupil, he would raise his cane threateningly and bring it down upon the boy's hand only to stop a few inches away. Bert never hit any boy and he was really a very good teacher, but I am sure some of us tried his patience at times.

Two of my teachers, Mr. Lewis and Mrs. Downs were calm and very encouraging in so many ways. Every year, near Christmas I believe, we used to put on a school concert. I never took part in it - I was much too shy in those days. Mr. Lewis used to fit all the stage scenes and the lighting in a very expert manner. He was young and energetic, in all a very likeable man and popular with all the boys.

There was a large cannon just outside the boys' classroom, a relic from the First World War. We used to climb on it until one boy fell off and got seriously hurt.

Empire Day was a great occasion. The whole school, boys and girls would sit in the open air and sing patriotic songs ending with Elgar's Land of Hope and Glory and the national anthem. That was when Britain had an empire to be proud of.

One of my best friends, in fact the best friend I had, was also an Ernie. Ernie Tummon and I went around together for a long time and I thought a great deal of him.

I was a slow learner but once I did learn the subjects, I never forgot them. I enjoyed composition and essay writing. Geography took me in my keen imagination to distant lands, and music lessons with a Mrs Dent were much enjoyed. One particular song I remember was 'Who is Sylvia'. I met Mrs Dent years later at my daughter's school open day and said to her 'I never did know who Sylvia was'. She seemed amused at this remark.

These next recollections may seem trivial events to the reader, but for me, they were important things and would have a profound influence on my life.

Once a year we would have a visit from someone from the William Harvey school. They gave lectures on the circulation of blood, rather a strange subject one might think, for an elementary school. I believe these lectures were sponsored by The Band of Hope, which used to be an organisation advocating total abstinence from alcohol. After the lecture we had to write an essay on the subject. If it was considered good enough, the essay would win a certificate. I loved writing and I won certificates two years running. (Incidentally, there is a hospital in Ashford, known as the William Harvey Hospital).

I have to admit that I did not excel at school. I think my shyness and lack of confidence was largely the reason for this. I did however reach the class known as standard 7(a), 7 being the top class so I couldn't have been that dumb. The teacher there was a Mr Cole, who taught history. He made it very boring and I hated it. Having grown up and seen historical plays and films, history has come alive to me in a way it never did then. Another teacher, Mr Head, who took Standard 5 class (which was one for those who were a little backward), came to our classroom to read a book in serial form. One such book was 'Mr Midshipman Easy'. He made it so interesting, mimicking the various characters. He did it so well that when it came to the end of the chapter we wanted to go on and hear more, but he left it until the next session and we eagerly waited a week to hear more of the story.

My Certificate of Merit, at the age of 12

So, at the tender age of 14 I left school. Joe Coupland told me, by way of consolation I think, that my English and spelling capabilities were above average, but I did not receive a scholarship. Even if I had my parents could not have afforded for me to go on to further education. We were required to get a job and bring money into the family. So, with school behind me I faced the daunting task of earning my living.

Before I go on to the next stage in my life, I must mention another important part of my upbringing. My introduction to religious teaching and its values, alas not held by many in these modern materialist times.

Chapter 2
Religious Influences / Affairs of the Heart

As my mother was a devout Christian and a Salvationist, I was sent to Sunday School at the little Salvation Army hall in Milton at the corner of Kingsmill Road. There I learned the familiar Bible stories about David and Goliath and Jesus Christ's brief life in Palestine. The visual aids used in our classes included a sand table. This was a large table with sides about six inches high containing sand to depict the desert scenes of Biblical times. Cut out figures and tiny models of eastern houses brought these old stories alive for me. It was a good introduction to my religious education and I can remember to this day those Sunday mornings spent in the classroom above the main church hall.

When I grew older, I attended the services, enjoyed listening to the band and hearing many enthusiastic preachers. On occasions there was a visit by a special preacher and I recall one who gave a very moving account of mission work in London's poorer districts. His vivid descriptions of the conditions in which many people lived in the city and their despair moved me to tears.

I was about seven or eight years old when one day at school I met my friend Ernie Tummon, in the playground. He wore a gold coloured badge on his lapel. (It was a craze then for boys to collect all kinds of badges). Enquiring about it he told me that it had been given to him for good attendance at the Primitive Methodist Chapel just two streets away. I was curious and not a little envious, so I told him I would like to go with him and see what it was like. My mother did not mind it seemed as long as I was attending Sunday school.

To cut a long story short, I continued to attend the 'Prims' as it was called and soon made friends there. My mother had connections there also, for she attended a women's meeting there called the 'Bright Hour'.

Childhood Friend, Ernie Tummon

At the little Methodist Chapel in Church Street, I began to make many friends, many of them who have remained so over the years and who I meet from time to time. I also grew to love the teachers who were so friendly and caring. The morning session was led by Mr. Bert Swan and Miss Howton. Both Bert Swan and Miss Howton were ideal teachers of young people and I think of them with affection. Mr. Swan was a foreman in the nearby Kemsley Paper Mill. It seemed that every other person in the area was employed in paper making in this mill or the second one in Sittingbourne. Papermaking was a thriving industry. Edward Lloyd, the owner of the mills had also built a garden village of modern houses for his workmen, one of the first of such factory villages built across the country. Complete with leisure facilities Kemsley village was a credit to Mr. Lloyd.

On the wall, behind the platform in the Sunday School hall, were two large hymn rolls which could be hoisted up for all of us to read as we sang. I can only describe them as being like oversized reporter's notebooks. The hymns were printed on large sheets of paper, each roll containing about 50 hymns. In the afternoons on Sundays we would gather into individual classes, each with our own teacher. Mrs. Selena Witts, a very strict indomitable lady, was the Sunday School Superintendent. She was assisted by her son Gordon who, on his mother's death took charge of the school. They both exercised a very caring ministry with all kinds of young people from various backgrounds. They took a personal interest in our religious upbringing. To them it did not matter if a child was poorly dressed or dressed in patched or torn clothes, even if they were not particularly clean or had runny noses. I think of Gordon and his mother with much love and admiration. I never realised at the time in my early life what an influence Mr. and Mrs. Witts would have on me.

At the age of 14 I was asked to take a class of my own of boys of 10 to 12 years old. I felt I was privileged to be asked to do this. Although I did not feel really suited to the job, the superintendent seemed to think I had a gift of some kind. I joined a Junior Christian Endeavour group under the leadership of Mrs. Witts. Members were expected to take turns in presiding over the meeting, being able to read a lesson and sometimes being asked to write a paper on a suitable biblical subject. We were also expected to take part in what was known as chain prayer. This simply meant each pupil praying one sentence and the person next to him or her doing the same, until all had made their contribution. All of this was very good training and gave us confidence in leading worship. Later I progressed to the senior section of Christian Endeavour and with others attended their meetings. We were all kept very much involved in the church. Sunday for me meant attending school at 10am, followed by the Sunday service at 11am. In the afternoon there was the class teaching and at 6.30pm I attended evening worship. This was the pattern of our life for many years, enjoying the friendship and worship of the church. By this time, I was about 16, many of my friends, the boys in particular, had left the church and I realised that I was the only boy of my age left. Ernie Tummon left to join the Congregational Church nearby.

It was during this time that my Uncle Charles, who was my Grandmother Taylor's son, said he would teach me to ride a bicycle. I had never thought of it and we could not afford one in any case. He gave me a bicycle and I was soon cycling into the countryside – it was a lot more enjoyable than running alongside with a steel hoop. I began to enjoy the thrill of riding along country lanes so quietly. I cannot remember exactly what happened but not many weeks after this incident I began working at Bobbing Court Farm and I always walked to work every day. Perhaps I just had the cycle on loan but it gave me the desire to buy one when I could afford it.

Meanwhile I continued to attend Milton Regis Methodist Church where I had already made many friends. These I believe were some of the happiest times of life, discovering things and people and girls!

I felt I was very lucky. Though still a little shy, I had the pick of girlfriends and made good friends with most of them in turn. I also, as a teenager, had many a heartache. I suppose because I took life and love much too seriously.

I had a crush on a girl named Iris who used to play the piano for the afternoon sessions of Sunday school. I wrote a note to her asking if she would go out with me. It was intercepted by her father who thought I was getting a little too familiar or serious at our age and promptly ended the affair. Thinking back, I was perhaps getting too serious, but I was very disappointed. Another girl who had dark curly hair, Ruby, also attracted me and we went about together for a little while.

About this time, I was 16 years old, I used to love cycling, usually on my own. A neighbour of ours who had a sister in Crawley, Sussex, asked me if I would like to spend the Easter weekend with her and cycle there. I said I would. It is about 60 miles from Milton so on the Good Friday I set out for the long ride from Kent into Sussex via Maidstone, Sevenoaks, Redhill and finally south to Three Bridges and Crawley. (There was, I believe an airstrip near Crawley. This has now become a major international airport which we know as Gatwick). Equipped with a little money, a Macintosh and tools in case of a break down, I set out. It was a beautiful ride through the Weald of Kent away from the noise and fumes of the town and I still enjoy the peace and tranquillity of the countryside. After a pleasant weekend, I began the journey back on the following Monday, returning across country, by way of East Grinstead, Tonbridge and Tunbridge Wells. I had arranged to meet Ruby at her house in Crown Road at 3pm. When I reached Tonbridge it began to rain, but I continued to cycle in spite of it. By the time I reached Tunbridge Wells it was really raining heavily, but I had a date to keep, so I kept going. The weather got worse and by the time I got home I was thoroughly drenched. I did feel a sense of achievement however, for I completed my journey and arrived just as I had planned, at 3pm in the afternoon but in no way in a suitable state for a date. However, when I arrived at Ruby's house she took one look at me in my dishevelled state and shut the door, tearing up a photograph of me I had given her, and throwing it onto the pavement. Soon after this Ruby and I did not go about together quite as much.

Ruby had a friend named Jean who she had known since they were small and often the three of us would walk out together. I discovered a day or two after my cycle ride that Jean had picked up the pieces of the photograph, taken them home and tried to stick them together again. This did my ego a power of good!

On one occasion me Jean and Ruby went for a walk through what was known then as 'The Meads' along a footpath to the village of Bobbing. There were springs underground there which often flooded in those days. The Meads is now the site of many new homes. There was an orchard on one side of this footpath; the trees loaded with ripe apples, which looked so tempting to us. With a kind of bravado and a desire to impress Ruby and Jean I said I would reach over and get some fruit for them. There was barbed wire fencing off the orchard but undeterred I climbed it to reach the fruit. Unfortunately for me my trousers got caught on the barbed wire and I was afraid to move either way in case I ripped them. After a struggle I managed to climb down, but not before I had torn the seat of my trousers causing me some considerable embarrassment, and minus the prize. I went home with a large tear in my trousers and on reaching home tried to hide the disastrous results from my grandmother, who I lived with at the time. I have to admit to being a bit conceited but this incident dented my pride. Ruby and Jean though were highly amused.

Jean Wellard was a plain looking girl at 14 years old (I was about 16). During this time I got to know Jean and discovered that she had taken a liking to me. Jean was one of a family of 12 children and consequently had none of the advantages that Ruby had, and I think she felt it very much and had an inferiority complex. Jean was a quiet, innocent girl, different entirely from Ruby. There was something about her that immediately attracted and appealed to me. We began seeing each other quite a lot and I would walk her home in the evening. Because we couldn't bear to leave one another we used to stand in the front porch at her house until her mother (Mrs Wellard) shouted for her to come in, because it was getting late. I used to be really frightened of her mother but found later that she was really a very kind person. I couldn't have been too bad an influence on her daughter, for sometimes later she would invite me into the front room. The front room was the 'holy of holies' of many homes. Only used perhaps once a year, though at times, the man of the house was allowed to have his meal here after a hard day's work. (Men generally did the hard work and were treated with respect being the 'head of the family'. I believe the women worked much harder bringing up us children, keeping the house clean and so on). To be invited to the front room was an honour and a privilege.

Although I did not realise it at the time, this was the beginning of a relationship which was to continue for many years and blossom for both of us. Jean was a very sensitive girl and I could so easily unwittingly offend her. Our little quarrels kept us apart at times but we always made it up and somehow, our friendship became stronger. I believe that often little crises bring people together in a real way.

It was about this time that Gordon Witts and his mother at Milton Methodist Chapel took a special interest in me. I had written more than one paper for the Christian Endeavour meetings, and one evening Mrs Witts said, 'You know, Ernie, you ought to take a note to preach.' I immediately dismissed this idea from my mind, only too aware of my humble upbringing and the fact that I had only had an elementary education. The very idea of public speaking of any kind was, I felt, hardly a possibility. So I made excuses as regards my ability. But Mrs Witts kept on trying to persuade me and for a long time I pushed the idea from my mind. Eventually, after thinking about it a lot, I agreed for her to put my name forward to 'go on note' as the term goes, as a potential preacher. The term 'on note' refers to a person who might be a likely candidate for the office of Local Preacher. It is, however, just a testing time of about 3 to 6 months. If the person recommended does not feel the call to train as a preacher, he can discontinue this initial test.

Gordon Witts, Milton Methodist Chapel

So in the next two quarters of the circuit plan of preaching appointments, I was with experienced local preachers travelling around the various chapels of the circuit. It was a humbling and a little frightening experience for me. I still remember, with gratitude, men like Bill Bennett, Ernie Lawrence and Frank Whitcombe, who gave me confidence. I can refer to them by their Christian names now. Then they were 'Mr' to me and I had a great respect for them.

There was another person for whose friendship and advice I was grateful, the superintendent minister, Rev Frederick Pearn. He was a lovely, fatherly Cornish man, who on my first service with him at the main church, Wesley Church in Sittingbourne, announced that…'a new star had appeared in the firmament', and that star was me.

**Sunday School Group on Sheerness Beach
with Mrs Witts Senior in dark clothes (circa 1935)**

It was the practice then that the name of a person 'on note' did not appear on the plan of Sunday services. Instead a small star or asterisk was printed by the name of the preacher at a particular church. A reference at the back of the plan indicated the identity of the trainee. Looking back I remember the long walk in procession with the choir into the church, with the choir leading the way followed by Rev. Pearn, and then me, trembling in my shoes, and a steward, to complete the procession behind me giving me no chance to escape the oncoming ordeal. Then the walk up the many steps to the pulpit placed high above the congregation. I do remember that, afraid as I was, Frederick Pearn calmed my fears as I announced the number of a hymn. I did little else at this my first service in the 'mother' church.

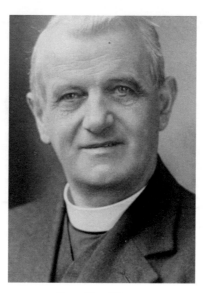

Rev. Fred Pearn

So began my career as a Methodist Preacher. I was about 16½ years old.

One evening Jean and I were sitting together in our usual pew at the back of the church when a steward, John Dutnall, walked along the aisle towards us. Reaching us he said 'Ernie the preacher hasn't turned up. Can you start the service?' I had never stood in a pulpit alone before and I was reluctant to do so now. Jean grabbed my arm 'You're not to go up there and make a fool of yourself', she protested. But John persuaded me and we went into the little vestry where I hastily selected 5 hymns. Having done so, I said a little prayer to myself and ascended the pulpit steps very nervously. To say that I was petrified would be putting it mildly. After the first hymn was sung, the preacher had not arrived as expected, so I composed a prayer, then announced another hymn and searched for a reading. Still no preacher. Another hymn and then it was time for the sermon. Somehow, I don't know how, I did preach one. I cannot recall the subject - probably one on 'creation', but I finished the service with a sigh of relief and not a little wonder. I cannot remember much about this experience, but I do remember that I felt that 'Someone' was giving me the ability to carry that service through.

I submitted this experience to the Methodist Local Preachers Department when they requested such stories to be published in a new publication on Local Preachers. The book was called 'Workaday Preachers'. I did not realise my contribution had been printed in the book until told by the sister of a preaching colleague I had known some years before. It was a pleasant surprise to see it in print.

To return to Milton Chapel Sunday School, as well as lessons on Religious education, we also formed a harmonica band. Mr. Swan was the instigator of this venture. There were about half a dozen or so of us boys and we had instruments from the smallest highest range to the largest deep-toned ones. I still have my chromatic harmonica but rarely play it. I could play it quite well but hardly of the calibre of the expert Larry Adler who played major classical pieces. The Church and Sunday School at Milton Methodist had a strong and lasting effect on my life, and also on Jean's.

I continued to see Jean quite a lot and we would often go to the cinema together. Rhoda, one of Jean's sisters, was very kind to me and did all she could to encourage and strengthen our friendship. She would often invite us both to her house to tea and showed a real interest in us. Rhoda was a lovely person and was always ready to give advice and help anyone with their problems. She did good work for the Samaritans and attended the Holy Trinity Church nearby where she was well liked. In fact everyone loved her because she was so genuine and caring. I have a lot to thank Rhoda for and her illness and eventual passing away in Medway Maritime Hospital in 1997 was a very sad time for the family and all those who knew her. An old friend of mine, who I meet from time to time once said, 'Rhoda was a saint and she is sadly missed'.

Chapter 3
Work Before the War

I began my working life at the age of 14, at 6am in the morning, on a farm where my father had been employed for a number of years. Bobbing Court Farm, owned by Ernest Mackelden and his two sons was a mile away from my home. Every day I walked to work with my father. My job that first morning was in the packing shed of the large cold store where the previous year's crop of fruit had been stored. A team of girls repacked the fruit as it passed along conveyor rails from the cold chambers and fed on to sorting and grading belts. It was my job to lift the boxes and stack them on one side. Later in the day I helped load the sorted and packed fruit onto lorries for delivery to the London market. I was referred to by the men as 'young Ern' and because I was fresh from school, I was teased by the women, but I soon overcame this. They were a really friendly lot and I soon became one of the team.

The farmer's eldest son, Jim, a young man, six feet tall, oversaw the work. He had an arthritic leg but was quite active in many ways. He was, I discovered, no mean a cricketer and played for the local village team. The 'boss' himself, another Ernest, was a friendly man in spite of being a bit gruff at times. He treated his workmen and women fairly.

Pop Apps, the farm bailiff [3], was also a good man to work with. He always had a cheery and friendly word. He rode a motorbike around the farm, organising the work. The sound of the engine gave him the nickname of 'Pop'. It could be heard for some distance around the fields and orchards. He lived with his daughter Rose, in a bungalow next to the 'big house', Bobbing Court. Rose did the

---

[3] The farm bailiff was employed by an estate owner, and his main task was to oversee the tenant farmers making sure that rent was paid and farms were well looked after.

secretarial work for the farm I believe. She was a devout member and organist of the little Methodist Chapel at Key Street. All in all, these were happy days and I loved the open air and the countryside.

I was given a variety of jobs to do around the farm. Sometimes I was put to work entirely on my own. When it was cherry picking season, I was given the job of bird scaring. This meant having to walk up and down between the rows of trees, turning a wooden rattle. I don't think the birds were put off that much because they were back in the trees eating the ripening fruit as soon as I had left that part of the orchard. It was lonely work. I had no watch to tell the time and one day I arrived home an hour later than I should have. Thinking it was 5pm and time to leave, it was actually past six. I somehow later gauged the time by the position of the sun in the sky.

Sometimes 'Pop' would pass by on his bike with the cry 'Time you was orf young Ern', or 'I 'ope you've keeping them birds orf those cherries'.

The cherry trade was at its height then. Trees as high as 60 - 70 feet carried bushels of luscious red fruit destined for London markets. It has since become decimated as imported fruit from Europe has been allowed to swamp our shops.

I had been at Bobbing Court Farm for six months when my mother died. She had been suffering from cancer for two years and my brother and I used to hear her cries of pain from our little bedroom across the stairs. I loved my mother and I believe we had a peculiar bond, more than my brother or sister. At least, this is what I felt. We both loved the church and felt the importance of a Christian Faith. I felt much too upset to attend the funeral, but before this my Grandmother Taylor, who I later went to live with when Dad remarried said 'Would you like to see her in her coffin'. I felt too afraid but I did see her face as she lay there. I was glad I had seen her this way after all that she had suffered. I was so upset that I did not attend church for some time. For me the bottom of my life had dropped out. Mrs Austen, the caretaker of the chapel pleaded with me, but I did not return to church for some time. It was only when she stopped me in the street one day and said, 'Your mum would want you to continue coming to church wouldn't she?' That chance remark struck a chord deep inside me and eventually I went back to attending the little chapel where I have found so much love and happiness.

At Work aged 15 (1938) moving ladders while cherry picking

But to return to work - I used to love to climb high into the trees, picking fruit of all kinds and I quickly found the art of handling a large ladder of 40 - 60 rungs. It was all a question of balance really. One morning Pop said to me 'I want you to go ladder moving at a plantation in Grovehurst for a gang of women. You seem to have the hang of it'. I could only have been about fifteen, and felt a little proud that he had considered me sufficiently competent to bear such a responsibility, and it really was so. One had to be sure of putting the ladder safely into the branches so to bear the weight and also to reach as much fruit as possible in one 'set' as it was called. Moving a 60-ft ladder on a windy day can be a hazard but I was quite confident and the ladies trusted me.

Other tasks I remember were to help plant a long hedge with two Italian prisoners of war, who had been employed. On another occasion I remember planting young trees in a field at Stockbury with two older men. The weather was atrocious. It rained incessantly all the time for days. Then there was the annual mucking out of the bullocks' yard. Not a pleasant job at the best of times but of course necessary on a farm where there is livestock to care for. There were no chemical fertilisers in those days.

There is one memory that stays with me. My first experience of leading the horse at ploughing time. Being told to do this I was quite scared when I saw the size of the animal - a large shire horse that dwarfed me. I was to lead the horse with the ploughman guiding the plough behind. It looked, and it was, really an easy though tiring job. However I made one simple mistake. I turned the horse at the end of the furrow but led him from the wrong side. I should have been on the side opposite the direction of turn. Consequently, as the giant beast went to turn, his giant hoof came down on my foot. Fortunately, the soil was very soft and I had the presence of mind to quickly draw my foot away before the full weight of the horse fell on it. 'That'll larn yer', was the ploughman's remark when he found I was not hurt. I had learned a simple lesson about leading a horse. These were happy days on the farm. I loved the open air and the scents of the countryside.

Whilst I loved the open air and the work in the country, the wages were very low, so after a year or so I left the farm to work for a local florist in Sittingbourne High Street. David Denny was a kind man to work for and he seemed to take me under his wing. His wife and two daughters ran the shop and Mr Denny would go to the nurseries and Covent Garden market in London for flowers. On one occasion he asked me to go with him. I had never been to London before and greatly looked forward to the experience. 'Be at the shop at 5am', he said, 'we have to leave early'. I duly presented myself and Mr Denny said when I arrived, 'Come upstairs for some breakfast before we go'. I had never seen such a breakfast, eggs, bacon, sausages, and how I tucked into it, with Mr Denny amusingly looking on. In London I visited the various stalls selling fruit and vegetables brought in from the surrounding countryside, and saw the abundant supply of gorgeous flowers. Having loaded the van we returned home in time to display our flowers when the shop opened.

The Dennys also employed a girl to help in the shop. Betty was a very tall girl and she and the Denny's daughters used to tease me because I was still very shy. Betty and I became friends and the Denny girls would have liked to pair us up, but I never forgot Jean who by this time had become a steady, serious girlfriend.

On the morning of September 3rd 1939 war was declared on Germany. Troops had crossed the border into Poland in Adolf Hitler's claim for power. Our government had promised support for countries threatened by the Nazi regime and in spite of the message 'Peace in our Time' which Prime Minister Neville Chamberlain brought home from Germany, war in Europe seemed inevitable.

Attending morning service at our little chapel in Milton we heard the air raid warning sound at 11am for the first time. It turned out to be a false alarm. However, it was not many months after that we began to experience the fear of bombing raids in the South East. Air raid shelters were hastily built in gardens and town centres and everyone was issued with gas masks, in case such a weapon was used against the population.

One particular night, after I had taken shelter with my grandparents at 21 Milbourne Grove, we heard the whistle of a bomb which seemed too close for comfort. There was no explosion, just a loud thud. We discovered in the morning that the bomb had landed unexploded just below the row of houses where we lived. We were all evacuated until bomb disposal experts made the area safe for us to return.

So for about a week we found refuge with many others in a large hut, which was usually used by the Scouts. The Blitz on London became a nightly dread and often the German bombers, returning from raids on the capital, would unload unused bombs on towns on the way home to help them make a quick escape from our fighter planes. Many fell on Sittingbourne and although we were spared the horrors which faced Londoners, we felt we were in the front line, so to speak. We were, in our country, ill prepared at first for such attacks, but later when the Spitfire and Hurricane fighter squadrons were in action, many enemy aircraft were sent spiralling to their ignominious end. We cannot begin to measure the part these courageous pilots played in the 'Battle of Britain' as it was named.

During this period, children were evacuated away from coastal towns and villages to safe havens in the countryside until the threat had passed. Sources of intelligence warned of a possible attempt to invade the South coast. German forces by this time had occupied most of Europe and their armies faced us across the English Channel.

It was a horrendous time in our history. A battle for freedom, not only for us, but also for those countries that had been suppressed just a few miles away. Because of the threat of an invasion, the Local Defence Volunteers (LDV) was set up. This later became the Home Guard. It was in fact a civilian army prepared, at all costs, to defend Britain to the last man.

I joined the LDV and armed with a broom handle as my only weapon, did training in the Drill Hall in East Street. (This was later the Church of The Pentecostals). I had to go through an obstacle course as part of that training. This took place in the chalk pits south of the town where I remember having to scramble through pipes and barbed wire and scale high obstacles, spurred on by the commands of a regular army drill sergeant. To add to the realism, crack riflemen would fire live ammunition close to our heels from the top of the chalk pit. It was for us raw recruits, a baptism of fire.

To return to my work again I had been happy at the florists, but I looked around for something that would offer more financial reward and went to work at 'Roonagh'. Roonagh was the name of a large house in its own grounds, south of Sittingbourne. A garden/house boy was required to assist around the house and grounds. An older man, Tom Gilham, came once or twice a week to do skilled jobs. The lady of the house, Mrs Andrews was a nice friendly person who I took to straight away. Her husband Wilfred was the director of the local garage Pullens, in West Street and travelled to a business in London every day. Wilfred Andrews was also the chairman of the Royal Automobile Club and regularly drove a veteran car in the annual London to Brighton road race. There were three children of the family. Roy who was a few years older than I was (and who ran the farm at Grovehurst, which was owned by Mrs Andrew's sister), Barbara, and Jean, the youngest of the family.

I spent some happy years at Roonagh looking after the garden and mowing the very extensive lawns at the rear of the house. Often there were odd jobs to do in the house and I got to know the family very well. I was once in the large billiard room, at the rear of the house, tidying some cabinets which contained albums of old records. Suddenly I realised that Mr Andrews had entered the room and I was expecting to be told off for looking inside the albums. 'Have you got a gramophone Ernie?', he asked. I told him I had a portable one 'Well then, you may borrow them whenever you like. Take an album home and play the records'.

I still remember that the very first symphony I heard was Elgar's 1st Symphony, which was complete on six 78rpm shellac records. They were 12-inch discs with only 3 to 4 minutes music on each side. How I thrilled to the marvellous opening bars of this majestic music. Now I can listen to a modern stereophonic recording of it and imagine I am really in the concert hall listening to a live performance.

During my time at Roonagh the Andrews employed two housemaids. One was named Marjorie, with whom I renewed an acquaintance when we moved to Newington, and we often recall those days when we met at our church there. The maid that followed was much younger, about my age, and was I remember, a chubby girl with a ruddy complexion. She told me once that she would go out with me if I volunteered for the Air Force. She must have had some effect on me at the time for I did volunteer and went to Chatham for the necessary medical examination. Later I travelled to London for intelligence tests and also tests in an aircraft simulator. I emerged from these tests with good results and a 'Good luck in your flying' from two high ranking RAF officers. However, all this was to no avail. I was not accepted.

One day Mr Andrews asked me if I would like to assist the painter in Pullens garage. So it was that I prepared cars for re-cellulosing with John Vallance, the painter. I rubbed my fingers raw in doing this because it meant getting a clean smooth surface on the body work, finally having to rub wax paste into the final coat of paint to give a highly polished finish. Wilfred, however, wanted me to spend every Friday in the garden at Roonagh, mowing the lawns and trimming the borders and so on, so that they looked smart for the weekend. I enjoyed doing this very much.

Mrs. Andrews used to give me little jobs apart from the garden. Sometimes she would ask me to cycle to her sister's farm at Grovehurst, two miles away, to collect fresh eggs for the kitchen. I enjoyed this because I was keen on cycling, having always liked the open air. Other times I would do a little shopping for her on the way back at the Co-op stores in Park Road, and collect pork sausages from Frank Whitcombes' butchers' shop in West Street. Mr. Whitcombe specialised in pork of very good quality. Mr. Bushel, a clerk at Pullen's garage, I discovered later, referred to me as the 'Sausage Boy' and as I was still a young teenager, I was teased by many people. I was in later years, to enjoy the friendship and encouragement of Frank Whitcombe for he was a senior Methodist local preacher and a very kind person in so many ways.

By this time I had begun to compose sermon material in my initial training as a Local Preacher. Barbara, the eldest daughter, said she would type it out for me and the family showed genuine interest in my studies. I discovered that George Andrews, a relation then passed on, had been a member of the Wesley Methodist Church in Sittingbourne.

At the garage I continued to work in the paint shop and I became skilled enough to paint the lining on a dairy van belonging to Mr Moss of Bredgar. Primrose Dairy was the inscription on the sides.

Here I met a Mr Harding who told me that he was a distant relative. He was an electrician for the firm.

I often did fire watch duty at the garage, which meant being on duty all night. I watched many a dogfight between our own Spitfire fighters and German bombers returning from London after a night raid on the capital. They would often jettison their remaining bombs before fleeing back to their bases in Germany.

Chapter 4
Call up and Life in the Army

In September 1942, six months after my 19th birthday, I was called up for service in the army. I was commanded to report to Maidstone barracks for initial training and this was to take 6 weeks. It involved square bashing, i.e. marching and drilling on the parade ground and roadwork, which was simply running, sometimes in physical training (PT) kit or full pack. All of us became physically fit. I remember the sound of the bugler, outside our barrack room window sounding Reveille every morning at 6am. How we cursed that sound.

An amusing incident comes to mind. As we filed along to be issued with our army kit when we arrived as recruits, a man in front of me was given his kit. 'Two mess tins, one brush, one comb', barked the sergeant. 'No brush or comb' said the man. 'One brush, one comb' repeated the sergeant. 'You will have a brush' began the sergeant when the man took off his hat to reveal a bald head. 'I don't need them' he broke in. Clearly angry and undeterred, the NCO repeated 'One brush, one comb, drawers cellular, two vests cellular, 3' etc.

Every morning we formed up on the parade ground in front of the barracks for drill. I had then, a thick mop of dark, curly hair and had difficulty in keeping my forage cap on. The drill sergeant became quite annoyed with me because of this and bawled out a few choice words for all the squad to hear 'Keep your b---y hat on curly or I'll make you pick up all the studs off the boots after parade' and also he barked, 'git your b---y air cut'. The regimental barber eventually did a good job at shearing my head, leaving only about ½ an inch of hair all over. One morning after breakfast, we were to do 'road drill'. I remember it was an icy winter's morning and we had to dress as for PT i.e. shorts, vests and slippers (known as plimsoles these days). Our run took us along the towpath of the river Medway that runs through Maidstone. Arriving at some point along this path we thought we were going to be ordered to jump into the frozen waters. Ordered to about turn, we all breathed a sigh of relief, cursing our ferocious sergeant who seemed to thoroughly enjoy making us suffer. Such was my indoctrination into His Majesty's Services. I groaned at the prospect of further training such as this but looking back now, I do not think it did me much harm.

Call up for the army, Maidstone Barracks 1942

We all had the usual vaccinations and they could make you feel a bit groggy for a few hours. Consequently everyone was confined to barracks for 24 hours afterwards. However, on this particular day the Methodist chaplain paid a visit and invited me back to his manse[4] for tea. Of course, he had to get permission for me to leave the barracks but this proved to be no problem. Although I did not feel too well, I appreciated the occasion and was later asked to conduct a service at one of the rural chapels of the circuit.

The six-week initial training came to an end and there followed intelligence tests and passing out parades. All the new recruits were asked what branch of the services we would like to be posted to. I offered to join the Royal Corps of Signals but when the actual postings appeared on the notice board, I found that I was to be sent for further training to the Royal Armoured Corps, based at Catterick Camp, North Yorkshire.

**58Z Squad, 601 Training Regiment, Royal Armoured Corps,
Catterick Camp, Yorkshire Feb 1943**

---

[4] A house provided for a minister of certain Christian Churches.

Catterick was known as the Aldershot of the North. Building at the garrison was still in progress and the site was muddy and bleak. One person ironically called it the last place on earth that God had made. The brick-built hut, which was to be home for the next twenty-one weeks, was accommodation for forty men. Another man and I were the only new arrivals from Kent among 38 Scotsmen. At night the air buzzed with snoring like the inside of a beehive, but we all got on fairly well together.

I discovered early on that members of one of the popular big bands of the day were also in the camp. The sound of 'White Christmas', a popular hit of that time played by Ambrose's band echoed across the camp. It was the age of the big dance bands such as Henry Hall, Billy Tenant, and Joe Loss, which were all the rage then. They would be doing the same training course as the rest of us and end up as members of the tank crew. We were issued with new uniforms with that peculiar smell that we had come to know, new RAC (Royal Armoured Corps) badges and a black beret. After the khaki forage cap, which would never stay on one's head, it felt a little strange at first.

The training began in earnest, spending hours on the parade ground and later classes for the duties of gunner/driver and radio operator. I found these classes very interesting. We took engines to pieces to learn the theory of internal combustion. I stripped down the various guns that I would probably be called upon to use in war, graduating to learn the operation of heavy tank guns such as the 75mm which was later fitted on our Sherman tanks. The radio classes I particularly enjoyed, although it did seem strange to have to use a microphone and Morse key communication. Our radio sets were known as '19' sets and were really three sets in one A, B and intercom. 'A' set was used for long distances, B for communication from tank to tank, and intercom for conversation between crew members inside the turret. I found it reassuring when in battle in Normandy later to know that we were in communication with others of the regiment and knew what was going on in our area. I became fascinated with radiotelegraphy and anything to do with radio. We also had to learn the duties of tank commander in case we were called upon in an emergency to lead a troop of tanks. I found the latter extremely interesting. I went on battle manoeuvres on the North Yorkshire moors and driving over the West Yorkshire dales was an exciting experience seated inside a Churchill tank. Gunnery practice took place on the remote moors of Fylingdales.

For those of us not taking part, it was our duty to man the entry to the moorland paths to prevent hikers from wandering into the range of the gunners. I well remember being posted with haversack rations at one point on the moor with only the sheep and the sound of the wind for company from 5am until 4pm. I took the opportunity to write notes. I was still in training as a potential Methodist preacher and the solitude and peace of the moors was, in its own peculiar way, inspiring.

At the end of 21 weeks we were trained as tank crews. There were the 'passing out' parades and the final preparations for posting to our regiments. I passed out as a Class III radio operator and wore my 'sparks' on the arms of my uniform with not a little pride because all in my class had done very well.

We had to have achieved a pass mark of 16 words a minute in sending and receiving Morse code messages. Our instructor, determined to get us through, had told us we were only doing 14 words a minute. Actually, we passed at 18 much to our amazement and delight. So I was a trained radio operator and ready to join my first permanent regiment.

I was subsequently posted to the 23rd Hussars, which was based at Newmarket. We lived in Nissen huts about a mile from the town. It was interesting on off duty hours to see the racehorses being exercised. Because the C Squadron Commanding Officer, Major

Blacker was an ex-jockey, the regiment were given the chance to see the 2000 Guineas. I had never been to a racecourse before and it was quite exciting. To see the horses and jockeys pounding round the course in their brilliant stable colours was a thrill.

After receiving wireless operator 'sparks'

A friend standing next to me asked, 'Which horse do you fancy?'. 'Well', I said, 'Herringbone looks a very good bet'. I didn't place a bet on him, but later we watched in amazement as Herringbone passed the winning post first.

As I always tried to do at a new posting, I found the local Methodist Church in Newmarket and attended the evening service. There was only a small congregation but afterwards a middle-aged couple approached me and asked my name. When I told them I was a Methodist myself they seemed interested and invited me back home for the evening. This was the first of many visits to the home of Mr and Mrs Hodge. They were a nice couple living in a street, which they said, was situated on the borders of Suffolk. They had two daughters, Irene and Jean. One evening I stayed too late to get back to camp and was invited to stay the night. This was quite all right as long as I was able to report to camp at Chippenham before 6am, or 0600 hours as we referred to time in the services. I was late in arriving at the camp but still thought I could get past the gates without being spotted. There was another man who had also stayed out. We were not so fortunate and we were both hauled before the C.O. for being A.W.O.L[5]. Suffice it to say that we both got off with just a warning. The training went on. We then just had one or two Matilda and Valentine Tanks, with 2 pounder guns and not much else. They became our training vehicles. Better machines would arrive later.

During those weeks at Chippenham Camp we went on one or two manoeuvres in the area. The use of dummy tanks made of wood and painted with the usual camouflage colours was a tactic that was tried. These possibly could be employed in battle to fool the enemy, but I don't know if they were ever put into operation. Some members of the regiment were sent out on adaptability tests of various kinds. I, with several others, was driven about 20 miles away into the country, given a map and told to make my way back to camp by the quickest route. Others had a more interesting challenge. They were ordered to get to London by whatever means they could, collect certain articles to prove they had visited designated places and return in three days. The objects were, for example, a London bus ticket, a garter from a dancer at the Windmill Theatre or a copy of a London newspaper. The Windmill Theatre incidentally boasted that it was the only theatre in the capital that never closed during the war. It was famous for its Tiller Girls, whose dance routines were so meticulously performed. Another activity between training was to cultivate the little flowerbeds in front of each troop Nissen hut. The competition was fierce but friendly.

---

[5] A.W.O.L. - absent from where one should be, but without intent to desert.

We were suddenly informed one morning that plans were being made for a possible embarkation for service in North Africa. We were kitted out with tropical clothes but it turned out to be a false alarm. We were told the advance party had left, but orders were changed immediately and we continued with manoeuvres and learned a little about battle tactics. The area north was very flat and wooded and we were called on one occasion to fight a forest fire which threatened several villages. During this period new recruits arrived and soon the regiment and brigade were complete. The 23rd Hussars consisted of entirely 'green' untested troops and were joined with another regiment, the 16/24 Lancers and the 3rd Royal Tank Regiment which had fought in North Africa forming the 29th Armoured Brigade, which was part of the 11th Armoured Division. We were fortunate to have a fine leader, C Squadron Tank Commander Major Blacker, who was a real gentleman and liked by all the men.

In the summer of 1943 the whole brigade moved to Bridlington, where we were billeted in houses from which families had been evacuated. It was much more comfortable than the Nissen huts of Newmarket and battle scenes continued to be acted out on the North Yorkshire Moors.

I became very involved in the many activities in the town when we were not on the moors. At the Spa Theatre members of the forces were invited to compere gramophone recitals. I was asked if I would be able to present an evening of classical music. I remember sitting on the stage of the theatre with a record player and a selection of music and enjoying the evening with an audience of about 50 servicemen and women sitting in the stalls. These recitals were very popular with many people stationed in the town.

I attached myself to the Quay Methodist Church in the centre of the town and soon made many friends.

Slarks, Redman, Bailey, Stone, Beatty, Gibson, Dixon, Jury,
Hewitt, Griffen, Sgt Jackson, Sgt McIntosh, Robson, Lt Poole, Kendall, Cook, Horsefall,
Torr   Reading   French

5th Troop, C Squadron, 23rd Hussars, Bridlington Yorkshire 1943

On the first morning there I told the minister that I was in training as a local preacher and I would be willing to take services if needed. His stern reply was 'Where's your credentials?'. 'I haven't any', I said, 'but if you get in touch with our minister Reverend Pearn in Sittingbourne, he would tell you about me'. He must have done this for a few weeks later I conducted services in the country chapels of the circuit. It was good training, which gave me more confidence. I conducted services at one or two of the moorland village chapels as well. A taxi was hired to take five or six of us preachers dropping us off at various places of worship. Afterwards, we would all be collected and returned to the town. If any of us had to wait for the taxi, we would be entertained at the home of a steward who lived nearby. On one occasion I remember cycling out to an appointment in the snow.

At St John's Methodist church in the old part of the town there was a youth club to which I became attached. The young minister there,

Rev. Douglas Morale, took a keen interest in young people. I became quite friendly with a girl named Margaret who was a little younger than me. Margaret Howton was a lovely natured girl who I believe had a particular liking for me. I have to admit that I grew quite fond of her (here we go again, another girl friend, but we were no more than friends). It is nice to find friends in different places. Margaret was petite, if one can call her that, and she had a charming lisp which attracted me.

During the off duty moments I had in Bridlington, I acquired some interesting books by the onetime president of the Methodist conference, The Reverend Leslie Weatherhead; a brilliant speaker, writer of books and also a gifted psychologist with his own clinic.

Through a friend of Margaret's, who attended the Baptist Church, I was invited to conduct a service in her church. It was held in the schoolroom and I remember that, to my horror, my sermon lasted about 30 minutes. I could not judge the time because the clock was on a wall behind me. Suffice it to say that I was not asked again, but I like to think that it was not because of the length of my address. On some evenings there would be dances at the Spa Ballroom which was part of the entertainment complex on the promenade. I had never learned to dance, nor felt the desire to do so, but Margaret persuaded me to go out on the dance floor. With the lights out I was quite content to shuffle around but when the spotlight beamed on us I took fright and ran for the side of the hall. I have always felt very anxious and even in my preaching career, have never quite conquered my shyness.

I soon developed a liking to this North East seaside town. The people, though perhaps abrupt, were kind-hearted and warm in their welcome for us of the 23rd, far from home. An elderly couple, Mr and Mrs Carter at the main church in the centre of the town invited me home on several occasions. Mr Carter was particularly abrupt which I found was a typical Yorkshire trait. I soon learned, that in spite of this, Yorkshire folk are very hospitable and friendly and I warmed to their kindness. When Jean met them during our honeymoon in Bridlington she was not so impressed, but then, she did not know them as well as me.

I have never ceased to have a soft spot for the people of Bridlington. I made many good pals in the regiment too and when off duty we would go into the town at weekends. We used to get up to all kinds of pranks to amuse ourselves. Simply looking up into the sky would cause passers-by to do the same, wondering what there was to see. Another joke was to start a queue. Everyone queued for something or other in those days. Five or six of us lads would stand behind each other outside a shop until, sure enough, people would join it, thinking it might be something special on sale. Many things were on ration and when certain things like fruit from abroad were in stock, the shops would be full, like a January sale is these days. When about ten or more had tagged on behind us we would calmly walk away leaving people quite puzzled. They were just like sheep. Human nature is a strange thing I've discovered.

We had our own regimental magazine called 'The Turret', which supplied us news of events, such as squadron football matches, or Ensa[6] Concerts and so on.

During our stay we did all sorts of exercises, learning how to seal our tanks in case we had a 'wet landing' on a foreign beach and polishing the skills for which we had been trained for so long. One morning the squadron was formed up along the harbour wall to practice survival in the sea, should we need to face such an emergency. We had to line up along the wall and when our turn came, we were ordered to jump the 15 - 20 feet into the water below, where rescuers waited to drag us from the sea to safety. I was dreading my turn, as I could not swim at all. Just as the man

---

[6] Entertainment National Service Association, was set up in 1939 to provide entertainment to the armed forces.

in front jumped off, the sergeant called me out of the line for some reason or other. I do not remember what it was. But I did not have to make the anxious jump into the harbour after all and I was really relieved about this.

It seemed after a few months that something was about to happen as regards the progress of the war, for the order came for tank trials in the sea to test water proofing. This was necessary in case the regiment's tanks had to land somewhere in deep water. Also, we had visits from General Montgomery, and a Royal visit by King George VI and Queen Mary with the princesses, Elizabeth and Margaret Rose. We spent hours lining up to receive them, resplendent in our uniforms, brasses polished fit to dazzle. I found it an inspiring and emotional occasion, marching to the music of a military band and forming up along the grass verge of the road by our tanks.

We still did not know what was in the future but we knew something was in the wind. Meanwhile, we enjoyed our happy stay in the town, getting very attached to the place and the people. To fill the time some of the men were able to go up in a Lancaster bomber from Driffield airport and others had the opportunity to pilot a RAF launch along the coast to Flamborough Head. I chose the latter and to be at the wheel, supervised of course, and skim the waves at speed was a thrilling feeling.

The regiment was asked, (or was it ordered), for each man to give a pint of blood for the war effort. We all did of course, though some tried to chicken out.

We were all now fully trained tank crews. I was a radio operator in 'C' Squadron Reserve by this time and we had taken delivery of heavy American Sherman battle tanks. Schemes on the North Yorkshire Moors continued with our new machines, which were much roomier than the old Churchill tanks we trained in back at

Catterick. Each troop consisted of four tanks; three having a 75mm gun and the fourth was to be fitted with a new top-secret gun, the 17-pounder, with this tank known as 'The Firefly'. The normal 75mm dual-purpose gun had proved itself against the German Mark IV tank in the desert, but it was no match against the 88mm guns of the Tiger tanks of the German Panzer brigades. The new 17 pounder had a greater armour piercing performance than the 75mm and one was allotted to each troop. This had a much longer barrel and also had a flash eliminator at the end. I well remember the first trials of the 17 pounder, which took place near Fylingdales one afternoon. All the important people were present to see how good this new weapon was. A shell was shoved up the breach and on an order, the gunner put his foot on the firing button. To everyone's amazement the shell just plopped out of the end of the barrel and fell just in front of the tank without any explosion. There were some very red faces. The next attempt was more successful and later in Normandy we realised just how good this new gun was, in our efforts to knock out the dreaded 88s of the German Wehrmacht. Later in Normandy, the Sherman I travelled in was a Firefly, equipped with a 17-pounder gun.

The day finally came for the brigade to move. It was an awful wrench because many of us had made 'Brid' a home-from-home and there were many tears from the population who had been so good to us, especially some of the girls we had made friends with. So it was that after 6 months intensive training on the Yorkshire Moors we were ready for battle and we left Bridlington with many memories of our stay there.

Our destination this time was Aldershot. We were housed in the old cavalry barracks on the outskirts of the garrison. The barracks consisted of two floors, a basement where the crews' tanks were sited (previously these had been the stables of the cavalry horses) and the upper floor being living quarters for the men.

The final preparations to our tanks were completed. We were ready for the final orders, our destination still a secret, though everyone had their own private ideas. It was quite evident however, that our brigade would be going into action somewhere and the atmosphere was buzzing with much speculation.

At last the orders came; the main body of the regiment was to move to embarkation points. A few tank crews were to be kept in reserve to be called upon when needed. It was my lot to be posted to Eastbourne with two other reserve tanks and crews. The same applied to the other regiments of the brigade. When we arrived in the south coast seaside town, we found that similar reserves of the Guards Armoured Division were stationed in the same road. We occupied large houses near Beachy Head and just sat tight as it were, for further instructions.

To occupy the weary days some of the men painted pictures of 'Jane' the pin up girl of the time, on the turrets, or inscribed their wives or girl friends' names on the front of the tank. I remember writing 'Jean' in white paint edged with red on the front of our Sherman. Jean was the girl I left behind. I remember wondering if I would ever see her again. One morning we were told that our regiment, the 23rd Hussars were going on a march to Pevensey Bay, five miles from Eastbourne along the coast, and we were going to march with the Guards Division (or some of them). Guardsmen at that time had to be tall and really stepped it out in their marching. We thought we would struggle to keep up with them, but we did, to the Guards surprise.

One morning whilst walking in the town, I heard a strange noise in the sky above the housetops. It sounded like the engine of a motorcycle I remember. Then suddenly it stopped and a moment later there was a loud explosion. I discovered later that this was one of the latest weapons of the German High Command, the V-1 rocket (or doodlebug as it was known). We were to see many more as they were directed to the City of London, causing so much fear and damage to the population.

As the V-1 started to bomb London, it was thought a good idea to park a Sherman with an ack-ack gun on the turret on the cliff top and try to shoot these rockets into the sea before they reached land. It went badly wrong when the gunner swung round to hit a rocket as it passed over the cliffs. He swung the gun too far, firing a bullet into someone's bedroom window, causing havoc to a very distressed lady about to go to bed. She made a very angry official complaint to a senior officer. The gunner was reprimanded and let off for his error. The lady in question was not so forgiving and the men who witnessed the incident were highly amused. Such was our period of waiting for further orders on the cliff road, St John's, at Eastbourne.

The days wore on, with no orders from the War Office, so we were given 48 hours leave. Being only three and a half hours travel from home I made the most of it. I realised now that soon we would be moving on.

The day arrived and, in convoy, our tanks and crews travelling on huge great Scammel transporters, we headed north for London. I remember going along The Old Kent Road early in the morning, perched as I was in the turret of my Sherman tank, as I was acting as tank commander, with mixed feelings about the coming journey into the war. There were few people to see us as we approached the East End, and at the West India docks later, our tanks were loaded onto LCTs (Landing Craft Tanks) seven to each vessel. There was a small crowd of onlookers who cheered us on and soon with a wave to them, we were on our way down the Thames to the sea. As we passed through various locks en route, we threw children our loose change. 'We won't be needing that', we thought! Eventually we arrived in the estuary and anchored a mile or so off Sheerness for the amazing variety of ships to turn up. It seemed to get larger with every hour. For two days we stayed moored up as the convoy was finally completed.

Across the water, I spotted the creamy white tower of the Rio cinema in Broadway, Sheerness, where I had often been to enjoy the latest films, and wished I could get ashore and return home. We did not want to fight in this war, but we knew we had to. As the leading warships moved off, we turned our heads to Normandy and its beaches, and whatever lay beyond. Then we set sail across the Channel and the tannoy announced 'Your destination is Caen.'

The Allied armies, we learned, had invaded Normandy. Our Brigade, the 29th Armoured, was already preparing for the battle for Caen and we were the first line reserves to fill the places for those who inevitably would be killed or wounded.

Chapter 5
Normandy and Beyond

I crossed to the Normandy beaches about one week after D-Day. It was an uneventful crossing. A seemingly never-ending convoy of ships protected by naval frigates made up the reinforcement force, and because the invasion of Normandy had been achieved it was not necessary to observe radio silence. The sound of music echoed from the tannoy. It was the entr'acte from Schubert's 'Rosamunde'. Whenever I hear this music now, I am reminded of the short voyage into the war.

We landed in about three feet of water on the beach at Arromanches, code named 'Gold Beach', and hastily drove ashore making our way where mines had been cleared, to arrive at last at the outskirts of the village, Cruelly, which was to be our first harbour in France. It was my responsibility, as commander, to deliver the tank to the camp, which was a large meadow surrounded by high hedges for good camouflage. On the way we had to pass through apple orchards, and a mate of mine on one of the leading tanks caught his head against a low hanging bough of a tree and was seriously injured. He had to be taken to hospital even before he had seen action.

Thinking of this incident reminds me of the untimely and unfortunate death of a troop member who, on the voyage across the Channel insisted on going below deck where the tanks had been loaded on, and with the swell of the sea and slight movement of the machines he became trapped between them and crushed to death. We had been warned against such dangers but he chose to ignore the advice.

Passing through the orchards we had been warned also of possible booby traps concealed in the trees. The turret of a Sherman tank is very high and could be a good target. However, I never heard of any casualties.

There was a great deal of activity as fresh reinforcements arrived by the hour. Across the meadow where we were camping was a broken down, burnt out Sherman tank. There was a neat round hole outside the turret, the result I suspected, of a direct hit by a German 88mm shell. 'Have a look inside,' someone next to me said. I refused. It did not require a lot of imagination to visualise the scene inside. Two of the crew, namely the radio operator and gunner had been unable to bail out in time. I learned later that in an emergency the radio operator is the last member of the crew to get out. I thought of this and was a bit scared of a possible emergency that I might experience.

After a couple of days preparation, I was assigned to a troop and later joined the regiment at Caen. My squadron, C squadron, had just been relieved from the first battle, code named 'Epsom', when I, with other reinforcements, arrived at the 'harbour'. Owing to ferocious gales along the landing beaches during 19 – 22 June, Epsom had to be delayed. The regiment did not go into action until June 26th. With the supplies and reinforcements eventually getting through, VIII Corps, of which the 11th Armoured Division and the 15th Scottish Infantry Division were a part, were ordered to break out of the bridgehead. The aim was to penetrate the enemy positions west of Caen. These first five days in action resulted in 2 officers and 34 other ranks being killed, with 6 officers and 30 others wounded; 8 were taken prisoner. The strain of those five days showed on the faces of those I knew so well in C squadron, as I joined the regiment near the battered city of Caen. When the Division eventually moved forward into battle on June 26th, one writer of the 11th's history wrote 'those who witnessed it will always remember the shock of seeing for the first time one of the regiment's tanks go up in flames.

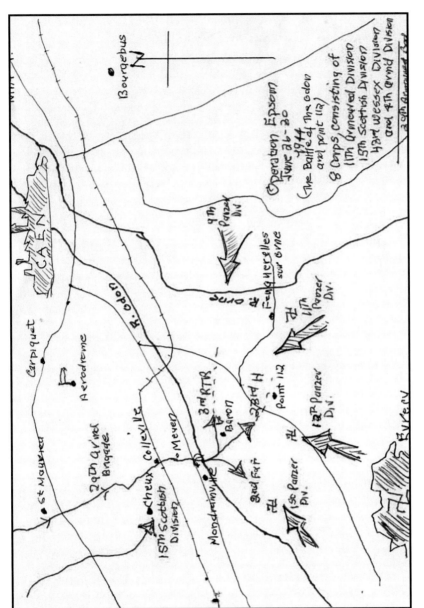

Operation Epsom

One moment an impregnable monster, the next a helpless roaring inferno containing one's best friends who we had trained with, on the wild, but peaceful Yorkshire Moors.'

As I joined the squadron, grim faced, overlooking the now devastated City of Caen, I braced myself for what was to happen over the next eight months. Few of us will forget that 'harbour' as we watched a massive bomber raid on the city below us. We had a front stall view. It was the prelude to an all-out attack with raids from the air and the burst of shells from battleships miles away, just off the beaches. From the heights of Caen, we looked down on the devastation as building after building crumbled. We had to admire the courage and tenacity, which the occupying German troops showed, as they fought fanatically for their positions. It took a month to clear Caen of the enemy and it took its toll of hundreds of young German soldiers.

After a few days rest, to take advantage of a hastily rigged shower, and to reorganise the squadrons, ('C' had suffered many losses), we were ready for the division's second offensive, code named 'Goodwood'. This was to be a thrust of three divisions, the 11th, the Guards and 7th Armoured, preceded by a massive aerial bombardment, north and east of Caen. So, on the 16th July, the 23rd Hussars, prepared themselves for battle for the second time. For me, it was to be my first real experience of war. At about this time with the reorganisation of the squadrons, I was transferred from a Mark IV Sherman to a Sherman Firefly.

The brigade moved west of Caen, to Raurey and we positioned our tanks in the open, behind the infantry. It was thought that the Germans would launch a counter-attack, but it remained fairly quiet. Our squadron tried a trial shoot of our guns against a German Panther tank, which stood nearby; its hull blackened by the explosion inflicted upon it. The results were depressing to say the least; the shells of the Mark IV Sherman 75mm guns made no impression upon it. Our Firefly 17-pounder gun proved more encouraging. I was glad that our tank had a 17-pounder gun fitted in the turret. I discovered, not many days later, that I would be busy loading it quite a lot in battle.

I must explain here that in Mark IV Sherman tanks, the radio operator sits on the left of the gun inside the turret. My wireless No. 19 radio transceiver, was positioned on a shelf in front of me. The gunner sat on the right, with telescopic sights to his front and the firing button between his feet on the floor. The tank commander sat on a seat, which was hinged just under the opening of the turret, from where he gave orders to the gunner to fire. In the Firefly the radio was relocated to the back of the turret in order to accommodate the much larger 17-pounder gun. The turret had been enlarged to accommodate the radio and I sat facing backwards to operate it.

I enjoyed operating the radio set because I always knew I could be in touch with what was happening at the front. I also had to record troop movements on a map in front of me. It was my job to keep the crew in radio contact and to load the gun with shells, which were about 30 inches in length stored around and under the floor of the turret. So, for the first time, I was to learn what 'going to war' really meant.

The second phase of the advance into Normandy, the Battle of Caen, code named 'Goodwood' was about to begin. The date was July 18th. There was an early morning mist and as it grew lighter, the whole of the 29th Armoured Brigade could be seen in battle order (or so I was told later, for I was busy inside the turret). The formation of tanks, guns and every form of assault weaponry were massed in a square mile of armour. An impressive sight I was told. I was to learn again what going into battle really meant. From the south of Caen, we moved across to the north east of the besieged city. Messages, reported to have been received by the German intelligence, suggested that we were a larger force than we actually were. We had to move fast to try and confuse the enemy. The sign of the Black Bull (the emblem of the 11th Armoured Division) was everywhere. However, the enemy were well dug in, deep below ground in four lines of defence, on the Bourguebus Ridge.

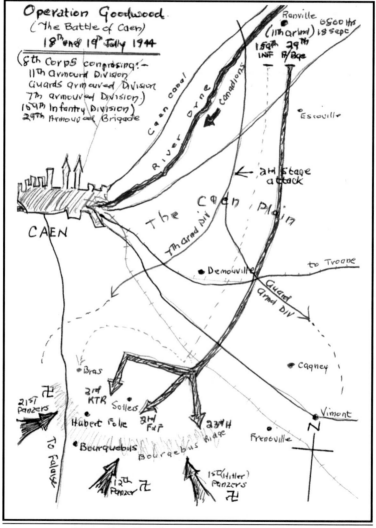

Operation Goodwood, The Battle of Caen

Prior to the attack we discovered that there was a minefield in our way, left by the previous units. This had to be cleared. The original plan was to advance three regiments abreast. This was now impossible. A small opening had to be cleared to allow only one regiment at a time, causing considerable delay in the battle. The enemy sited on their ridge could easily see us, but I believe were out of range. Having got all three regiments through the gap we then had to spread out and advance abreast. These things I learned later. Deep inside my 17-pounder Firefly I was almost unaware of the position, relying on my No. 19 set transmitter and radio receiver for any information.

As the mist cleared, we heard the distant drone of approaching aircraft; a massive armada of bombers to 'soften up' the enemy defences. Soon after, came the familiar throb of Marauders, Halifaxs and giant Flying Fortresses with Spitfire fighter planes weaving in and out among them. Later came the tremendous sound of explosions, as they unloaded their deadly cargo amongst the German tanks and guns way ahead.

So the order to advance sounded in our headsets and we moved forward, to do battle against Hitler's 21st Panzer troops. As reports of enemy tank positions were radioed to us, I plotted them on my chart with little swastikas, and a picture of our situation was built up. By this time the 24th Lancers had been replaced by the 2nd Fife and Forfar Yeomanry.

With the 2nd Fife and Forfar (F & F) tanks on our left and the 3rd RTR (Royal Tank Regiment) on our right, the 23rd Hussars followed in reserve. As we approached the first railway line, which ran from Caen to Troarn, there was little opposition. The second railway came into view, from Caen to Vimont, and we could now see that the ground beyond us was completely open forming a cup. Before this was the high ground of Bouguebus Ridge, where the enemy were firmly entrenched. Suddenly, from the Bourguebus

Ridge, the leading troop of F & F came under intense fire from 88mm guns of the German 503 medium tank battalion. The 3rd tanks on their right also fell victim to an onslaught of deadly accurate fire from dug–in Panther and Tiger tanks. Several of their tanks were seen on fire and blazing, their crews escaping from the burning hulks and running back to safety. The Brigadier ordered 23rd Hussars to assist the 2nd F&F, now being mercilessly attacked from all sides. Now the squadrons of the 23rd were also at the receiving end of the enemy's guns and nearly all their 75mm and some 17-pounder Firefly tanks were knocked out.

Amongst my first memory of the battlefield was the sight of burning Sherman tanks and those of the enemy, littered about the plain as we advanced. The corn was ripening and dust turned up by dozens of heavy vehicles hung like clouds about us. From my tiny periscope, only six inches by two approximately, I could see very little, but the deafening noise of screaming shells was enough to make me aware of the onslaught of enemy guns hidden in trees in front of us. Sergeant McIntosh, our troop Sergeant's tank was just in front of us, as we topped a hill on the plain. Somewhere to our right came the unmistakable crack of a Tiger tank's 88mm gun. One moment our troop Sergeant was giving frantic orders from the hatch of his tank, the next moment his body now headless was slumped over the turret. The shell had skimmed above the Sherman, severing the head from his body. Although I was unable to actually see this dreadful end of a member of my troop, I heard the account of his sudden calamity from reliable authority sometime later. I realised that in the event of a direct hit, I would be the last man to escape from the fragile safety of our steel fortress, being the furthest away from the opening hatch.

During the battle on the Caen plain, a glancing shell from an enemy tank, struck the base of the turret of my tank without exploding. For a very brief moment I quite expected our tank to 'brew up'. Fortunately for us, we did not. We were lucky, but it meant that our gunner was unable to traverse the gun, in effect rendering the mechanism useless. So we had to pull back to the REME (Royal Electrical and Mechanical Engineers) workshop for necessary repairs to be carried out. I had great admiration for the fitters, for their engineering skills and the speed they were able to complete vital repairs. Their motto was 'the impossible we do at once; miracles take a little longer'. It was not long before we were back in action with the squadron once again. We continued the next day after first light, to advance to Bouguebus Ridge in the face of horrendous fire which raked the squadrons.

As our gunner engaged an enemy target several hundred yards away, the empty shell cases clattered from the breach of the gun, filling the inside of the turret with the acrid smell of cordite, which was to become a familiar smell to us. Looking back now, I wonder how we were able to cope with such dangers that faced so many young men like me. The fields south of Vimont were strewn with the knocked out tanks of the Brigade. It was a disaster area.

We drew back at the end of another gruelling day, to previously occupied and consolidated positions, overlooking the village of Bras and Hubert Folie. Fifty percent of the division was out of action.

'Goodwood' proved to be a tough operation; our flail tanks at the start of the operation having to clear a path through a minefield which gave German gunners opportunity to pick off some of our Shermans. However, we were able to hold our position before Bourguebus, against terrible odds, although we failed to capture the Ridge. Whilst things did not go to Monty's (Field Marshal Montgomery) plan, we were able to hold the enemy at bay, so allowing the Americans to break through the area near St Lo in the west, and move up level with us south of Caen. This was my personal baptism of total war and I was fortunate to come out of it all unscathed.

As I said earlier the 23rd Hussars were 'green' soldiers with no experience of battle and there we were up against seasoned troops, such as the infamous 21st Panzer Division, who had a fanatical reputation. However, the 11th Armoured Division, of which our brigade was a part, were already gaining a reputation of their own. It seemed that the signs of the Black Bull on a yellow background, which was the logo we wore on our uniforms, were everywhere to be seen. Carpiquet airport, north of the city, was freed and I recall driving through the ripe cornfields, past the burning hulks of our own and enemy tanks.

The regiment stayed for a week at St Germain to fill the depleted ranks of tank crews and to plan the next phase of the Normandy offensive. We were to move our action from the eastern front to the west, near the town of Caumont. By this time, the Americans had come up from the Omaha and Utah beachheads, and the plan was to make with them on the right flank, a spectacular sweep south to take the main route from Le Vassey to Vire and then on to Falaise. This would completely encircle the area of Caen, cutting off the remaining divisions of the German Panzer groups. This was to be known as 'Operation Blue Coat' and was to prove the longest and bitterest battle of the regiment.

As we advanced, the Guards Armoured Division on our left flank, and the chewing gum boys, (as we referred to the Americans on our radios) on our right, the countryside changed from wide-open plains, to thick hedges and sunken lanes, the Bocage country. As we were to discover, very dangerous terrain, for one never knew what lay ahead.

It was the morning of 29th July. The front opposite Caument was held by a German parachute division, which was made up of tenacious fighters who were determined to give no inch of ground. The regiment reached Le Beny Bocage, after a few skirmishes in the very difficult country. Amid throngs of delighted villagers who greeted us with cheers, jugs of hot strong coffee and glasses of the local tipple 'Calvados', which is produced cheaply in this area of Normandy, we pushed on.

With Caen taken, the encircling manoeuvre took us further south and the battle continued to the distant ridges of Presles and Perrier, from where we were able to command a view of our final target, the main road from Vire to Vassey. My troop was in reserve again and we harboured in the town of Le Beny Bocage, with the headquarters (HQ) echelon. A, B and C Squadrons, with a company of the 8th Rifle Brigade, had probed forward, to test the German defences. The infantrymen of the Rifles, fought with us all through the Normandy campaign and proved good friends in many ways.

At this point, it might be useful for the reader to know a little of the tactics of an armoured brigade. A particular regiment of a brigade is not always in the spearhead of an attack. When the front-line troops are tiring and need relieving, a second regiment moves up between them to take the lead, and when it is deemed necessary, the third regiment passes through them to take their place. This applies not only to regiments, but also to squadrons and troops within those squadrons. A troop of tanks consists of four tanks. Five troops, one of which is a reserve, forms a squadron. I was in the reserve troop in the first phase of the campaign and continued in this troop.

In these situations, it will be appreciated that there are always units who are in reserve and prepared to move up and take over, when the battle gets particularly tough.

One morning the echelon was placed on alert. It was reported that an enemy tank had managed to get through the line and was about

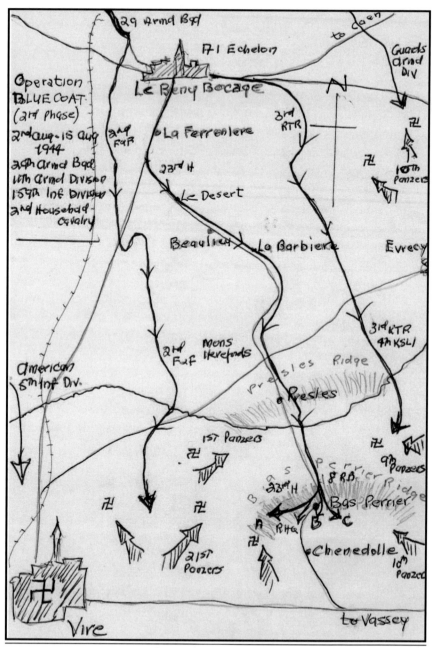

Operation Blue Coat

to attack. For several hours we were on watch but the information proved to be false.

The 17-pounder Sherman, in which I was radio operator, had engine trouble and leaked oil quite badly. I suppose that was the reason we were LOB (left out of battle).

Things must have been getting very bad at the front, just a mile or so away, because a day or two later our troop was called into the battle. The way to the hill at Le Bas Perrier, a dusty one, led through narrow country lanes, bordered by hedges and was also hilly in places. We passed signs put up by the engineers who warned 'Dust means shells', so that our progress was slow, although a Sherman can travel quite fast. The sight of rotting cattle, heavy with milk, became a familiar scene now in the Normandy Bocage[7] country. The stench of rotting carcasses and burning buildings filled the air. This type of country was dangerous to advance through, for we did not know what dangers the thick hedges hid from us. Quite often a hidden German 88mm gun would have a good view of us, and could easily reduce a Sherman to a burning hulk. The Germans nicknamed them 'Tommy Cookers.'

When I joined the forces, I was given a pocket New Testament. As we drove up to the hill, which our regiment was defending, I took it out of my pocket, opening it at random. The page fell open at the Letters to the Colossians. The verse that I read, St Paul's words to the early Church was, 'For I know what great conflict I have for you.' I had looked for words of comfort but instead they put fear into my mind as I thought of the immediate conflict ahead. Studying the letter years later, I discovered that the conflict referred to was not the reader's but Paul's concern for his friends at Colossae.

---

[7] Bocage: A French word to describe an area of countryside with thick hedge rows bordering lanes.

A battle was being fought on a small hill overlooking Le Bas Perrier. We arrived at the scene of battle, amid a thundering noise of heavy gunfire from our tanks and those of the German Panzer troops, who occupied the village of Le Bas Perrier, some 200 - 300 yards below. As we drove our tanks off the narrow lane, and up onto the hill, which the regiment was defending, the colonel shouted down the mike 'Who's that bl-y fool coming up on my right?'. He of course meant us. With confusion all around the hilltop and in the heat of the moment I replied 'Sergeant Jackson's reserve tank sir' I should have used the code sign to identify myself, but in the noise of gunfire and the chaos of our situation I forgot to do so. Apparently, we had exposed our tank to the marauding German Panthers who somehow had crept up on our positions. The CO did not want to lose another Sherman, or its vital crew, at such a critical stage of the battle. I was not reprimanded and the regiment was more than glad to see some reserves at such a time. There was chaos everywhere. It appeared that a German Panther tank had circled the hill to our right and was threatening 'B' squadron position. The battle lasted all the afternoon and as it grew dark the enemy had withdrawn to the safety of the village. A strange quiet descended on the scene for a while, to be suddenly broken by the demoralising scream of 'moaning minnies'. The German name for these multiple mortars was 'Nebelwerfers'[8]. They made a weird whining sound as they came through the air landing around us. This was to be a regular occurrence in the early evening, designed probably to let us know that they hadn't gone away.

Many stories could be written about the bravery, and fears we all experienced during the days to follow on 'Hill 224' as it was designated:

-   of the courage of our Medical Officer Captain Mitchell who continued tending the wounded under heavy gunfire.

---

[8] Smoke mortar.

- of my troop commander, Lieutenant Peter Robson, aged 20, who lost his life whilst trying to rescue the crew of a blazing mobile gun.
- of the rear-echelon lorry drivers, who late at night when things had quietened down before the first morning counter attacks, came up with fresh supplies of petrol for our machines and 'K'[9] rations. Also, the longed-for letters from home. In their soft vehicles they took many risks to keep us going.
- of the pilots of the little Lysander aircraft who acted as spotter planes, to direct our artillery fire over our heads onto German positions in front of us. Twice the regiment was cut off, when enemy tanks and infantry ambushed fitters coming up to do repairs, so isolating us from the echelon HQ miles behind us. Once it was for 24 hours, but fortunately supplies had already been safely delivered to the regiment and the wounded had been taken back behind the line for treatment in the field hospital.

Sherman Firefly, possibly in Holland

---

[9] K' rations were American packs which contained such food as tinned bacon, sausages etc which were of a high quality and eagerly received.

Such was the pattern of the next six days, as we held our positions on the hill. Towards the end of the week, as there was so little manoeuvring space on the hill, it was decided that A and B squadrons be withdrawn to Le Beny Bocage, leaving our C squadron to defend the position. Once again when the supply vehicles were coming up from the echelon, an enemy tank circled us cutting us off for an hour or so. Things appeared to quieten down by day 5, so our troop was ordered to go down to the edge of the village and investigate. As often the plan, soldiers of the 8th RBs (Rifle Brigade) travelled on the back of the tanks to patrol the area, once we reached Le Bas Perrier. We slowly made our way across the open ground that lay between us and Le Bas Perrier, expecting at any moment to be fired on, but all was quiet.

We reached the edge of the village and Sergeant Smith's tank probed further on to find the infantry. Suddenly, we spotted a tank almost hidden in the trees. We did not know if it was manned and just waiting the chance to lure us on, or knocked out and immobile. The sound of a rifle shot from a sniper pinged against the opening of our turret. Our fears were confirmed. From the hill, an order came on the radio to return to the squadron. The driver in my tank went to start the engines, but no sound came. Several attempts failed. I could not use the radio either. We were stranded, helpless and surrounded by German infantry, the barrel of our 17-pounder pointing at the enemy tank among the trees. Sergeant Smith in the forward tank, returning in response to the order to withdraw, found us. Under rifle fire my tank commander Sergeant (Fred) Jackson got out of our tank and helped secure the cable to Sergeant Smith's tank and Sergeant Smith slowly began to tow us back up the hill to safety. Our squadron leader had told us to abandon our disabled tank but I remember Fred saying, 'I am not leaving this tank for the Germans'. We all prayed that the tank in the trees would not open fire, but we had moved little more than a hundred yards when a shell exploded at the side of our tracks. After what seemed a lifetime, we all reached the safety of the trees on the top of the hill relieved to still be alive. Somehow, I cannot explain it, I felt in that dreadful situation that we were not alone. 'Someone' else was there with us on that lonely hill in Normandy.

Sometime after the war, when I received a copy of the history of the 23rd Hussars, I read that both Sergeant Smith, and my tank commander Sergeant Jackson, won awards. The Distinguished Conduct Medal for Sergeant Smith and the Military Medal for Sergeant Jackson.

On another occasion, one of our British Typhoon rocket fighter ground-attack planes, mistaking us for enemy tanks dived down upon us. Hastily we showed the yellow silk signal, which was used for identification, but too late. The deadly rockets thudded into the ground just a few feet away. As on various such incidents we breathed a sigh of relief.

The battle continued and in spite of heavy stonks[10] of shelling by the 25 pounder guns of 13th RHA (Royal Horse Artillery), directed on the village below, enemy tanks again and again managed to creep around our left flank and began to attack our remaining Shermans. Because there was not enough room on our small hill it was decided that all but C squadron should pull back in reserve position.

We felt at the time, that C squadron plus a troop of B, were left alone to hold on to the hill. But we had massive artillery back up and tank destroying aircraft that rocketed the enemy positions. We learned later that the 10th SS Panzer division, who faced us, had been given orders to take the hill, at all costs. In fact the German general, General Eberbach had reported to Field Marshal Von Kluge, his superior officer, that the 10th had captured hill 224. This was not true. The squadron was determined to defend our hill, to the last man if need be, so important was it to the whole plan of

---

[10] bombardment with concentrated artillery fire.

Operation Bluecoat that we held on to our position along the ridge. The enemy pulled back. The cost had been too high.

Eventually things did quieten down in the village below and the RB's (Rifle Brigade) confirmed that the enemy had retreated. Exhausted, tired and dusty we moved back to the safety of La Barbiere, where the regiment was resting. What a rousing reception we received as our tanks drove in and how thankful we were to rejoin our pals in comparative safety at La Barbiere.

These six days, were for me, the most horrendous experiences in the battles of the occupation of Normandy.

After three or four days we were refreshed and ready to advance again. We had now made a wide encircling movement driving north to Falaise. The enemy, outnumbered by advancing British, Canadian and American Divisions were attempting to escape to safer positions. The allied armies began a tactical advance almost enclosing the fleeing German troops. The circle was not quite completed, but at Falaise the trapped enemy infantry and tanks were pounded by gunfire from all directions. The slaughter was almost complete but some units of the German Wehrmacht managed to escape to fight another day. It was a horrendous massacre and the inglorious defeat of a great part of the German divisions, in what became known as the battle of The Falaise Pocket.

The regiment rested again at L'Aigle, washing some of the grime of battle off our bodies in a nearby stream, watched by a group of giggling French girls.

Shortly after this the 11th Armoured Division began, what has been described in newspaper reports, as one of the most spectacular advances of the Normandy campaign. Usually a tank brigade rests at nightfall, but this particular night happened to be a moonlight one and the order came to continue the chase, now that we had the enemy on the run. It was a truly spectacular advance, a bold spearhead of troops, guns and tanks probing deep into enemy occupied territory. So fast was the advance that the units of enemy troops were overtaken, they thought we were a long way back. Amusing incidents occurred too, like the German convoy who came out of a side road to join us thinking we were their fleeing comrades. At the town of Amiens, however, the Panzers put up some considerable resistance but the sheer weight of numbers of our forces pouring up from the south overwhelmed them. Just before we arrived in Amiens, however, our 17-pounder Sherman broke down again. As I sat by the roadside waiting for REME to come and tow us in for repair, I noticed an army ambulance, which drew up on the opposite side of the road. I was amazed to see Henry Hall (coincidently the same name as the famous band leader), a school pal of mine emerge from the cab and come to meet us. It was even more amazing to meet him again many years after the war, when an ambulance, this time from Medway Hospital, stopped in Church Lane, Newington, where we had moved in 1952. I recall saying to him 'Do you remember the last time we met'. It seemed incredible that our paths had not crossed in the years since that meeting.

And so the race began again, our destination being Brussels. I had hoped that our division would be chosen to retake Paris. That was the prize of the American 7th Army. We drove into the streets of Brussels, totally surprising the German troops and had great difficulty in getting through the teeming, excited crowds that almost blocked the streets. The population was ecstatic, climbing on to the turrets of our Shermans and throwing their arms around the crews. Being right inside I could only listen to the clamour going on above me and around me, but it was still an exhilarating feeling.

The order came to push on to Antwerp. The German forces intended to defend this important port at all costs, as once captured by the Allies, it was planned to be used to bring in supplies. From Caumont to Antwerp, 11th Armoured Division advanced 230 miles; the last 100 of these at the rate of 53 miles a day. So Antwerp was taken, and after our long and spectacular drive from Normandy we rested for a few days; tired and exhausted. The Allied targets were now the towns of Nijmegen and Arnhem. We switched our advance deeper into Holland, passing through Weert and Eindhoven, to be ready for Operation code named 'Market Garden'. A bold massive series of parachute landings had been planned to capture Nijmegen and eventually, Arnhem, and hold these towns until the Guard Armoured Division and we of the 11th Armoured Division could link up with them and drive into Germany itself.

One morning as we travelled in convoy, we watched dozens of gliders passing over us, on their way to take the bridge at Arnhem. It was an impressive sight and I shall never forget thinking how glad I was not to be among the paratroopers inside them. The plan turned out to be too bold, for the German army was ready for them and many of our men lost their lives in the attempt. It meant that we would not be advancing north. We harboured up at a tiny place called De Rips, in wooded country, to await further orders. While we were there, the Dutch supplied us all with boxes of cigars, a gesture of their pleasure at our presence on the scene.

Finally, orders came for us to move east towards the river Maas. The weather had become poor and it rained for days, making it difficult for our tanks in the marshy ground. We eventually made camp at Leunen, not far from the town of Venlo, and we were to remain there defending the position for six weeks. We were often under heavy artillery gunfire from the enemy, but we just sat and held our ground under orders not to fire our guns for fear of disclosing our presence in the area. It did no good for our nerves. In fact one of my mates lost his mind completely and ran amok and was killed. It was not at all a happy situation to be stationary, especially after our victory drive to Brussels.

Enemy patrols tested our defences by sending suicide squads into our lines. In the dark they would drop grenades into the turrets and when the order came not to sleep in our tanks we dug trenches in front of them. Even then troopers of the regiment were silently attacked. Those six weeks proved to be a nerve-wracking period and some minds cracked under the strain. Relief came in the form of a mobile cinema, or 3-day rest periods to Helmond for everyone in turn.

A few of the men's nerves had been severely tested, I being among them, and we were sent for a medical check-up to a hospital in Brussels. I was asked the stupid question, 'What is the capital of London?', by one of the doctors. This was to find out how bad our nerves or minds had been affected. I felt at that time in Holland that my nerves had been stretched like an elastic band, almost to breaking point. Thankfully, I regained my composure and was fit enough to return to the front.

I have read that in the First World War we would probably have been treated severely and considered of no use in action. Many of course, nerves shattered, refused to fight on and were shot. 'Monty' of course had more common sense and sympathy for his troops. He appreciated the strain upon his men and gave us a rest from action. I was able to re-join my squadron, strengthened in mind and body, to fight alongside those who had become some of my best friends.

And so the gruelling weeks along the River Maas, which separated us from German soil, continued. The incessant rain, which turned everything into a bog, proved a great hazard for our tanks. The Germans would plant mines in the trenches. When the German artillery opened up, one morning, one of my mates Les Cumper, jumped into a trench for shelter and a mine blew his leg off from the hip. He was a lively character and kept us amused by his supposed escapades with women, whenever he got the chance. He was flown back to England and survived the terrible injury.

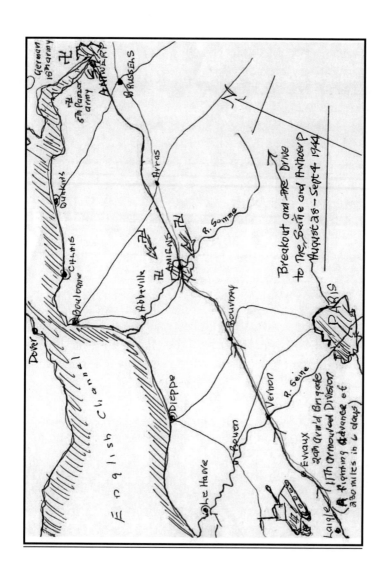

Breakout and drive to the Seine and Antwerp

78

THE ASTONISHING STORY OF THE 11TH ARMOURED DIVISION.

From Henry Standish, News Chronicle War Correspondent
(extract from News Chronicle, Wed 8 Nov 44)
-oOo-

Brussels, Tuesday.

One of the most remarkable features of the British Campaign
since D-Day has been the way in which some Divisions, hitherto
unknown to the public, have proved such efficient fighting formations
that automatically one expects to find them in the thick of each new
operation.

That is one of the reasons, of course, why the Army does not
permit identification of units and formations until some time after
actions are concluded.   Enemy Intelligence spends a lot of its time
trying to keep track of our 'order of battle', that is, which units
are where.

The Germans know, just as Field Marshal Montgomery knows, that
some of our troops are better for particular jobs than others.   We
cannot afford to tell the enemy anything that will help them to
estimate our intentions.

So there are many magnificent formations which are virtually
unknown to the public.   One of them is the 11th Armoured Division,
which in 134 days was out of contact with the enemy for only five
days.

I am now permitted to tell the story of this fine formation from
the time of its arrival in Normandy a week after D-Day until its
dramatic capture of ANTWERP on September 4.

Only the highlights of its many achievements can be given, but it
is a tremendous story.   For the 11th Armoured Division, which had its
first Battle Experience in Normandy, packed into 3 months more
experience and greater triumphs than many older formations have
achieved in long years of honourable service.

The 11th Armoured Division has all the advantages of sound
training at home and perhaps the greatest advantage of all - a
commander with a fine record of tank fighting in Africa.   He is
Maj.Gen. "Pip" Roberts, famed for his capacity to exploit every
opportunity afforded by a break-through of enemy positions.

Under his command it was inevitable that the Division should
arrive in Normandy thinking in terms of 'break-throughs'.   They had
hard and bitter positional fighting before the chance came really to
show what they could do.

Their Armoured Brigade won and held the bridges across the Odon
until infantry could get up to take them over.

They took Hill 112, which someone christened Calvary Hill, and
held its slopes and crest for 48 hrs until the crest became untenable
by shelling and mortaring.   The fighting round 112 was some of the
bitterest seen in this war.

There was an occasion when men of the Recce Unit had to get down
out of their tanks to fight as infantry.

In the end nobody was able to establish himself on the crest, and
only the reverse slopes could be held.

The brunt of the big operation South East of CAEN, when we broke
through the positions on which the enemy was hinging his whole front,
was borne by the 11th.

It was planned as a three Armoured Division operation, but so
great was the traffic jam at the three bridges across the ORNE that
the other Divisions were unable to give the expected flank support.

That day the 11th had many tanks knocked out.

The figure was reported to Divisional headquarters in the Middle
of an air raid when the Germans scattered anti-personnel bombs over
the Divisional headquarters and the rear echelon, causing a number of
casualties.   Fortunately, more than one-third of the immobilised
tanks were recovered the next day and quickly put back into service.

News Cutting 'Now It Can Be Told'

79

So, at Leunen, not far from Venlo, on the Dutch/German border we attempted to put on a cheerful face against the elements and dangers lurking in our stretch of 'no man's land'.

Quite unexpectedly the brigade was put on alert to move again. At first we did not know where we were going, but eventually we discovered our brigade had been ordered to move right back to Ypres in Belgium. When we reached the artillery lines on the way, an amusing incident occurred. A German general had been captured and wanted to know where the multiple artillery cannon were. In actual fact, this so-called multiple gun was a line of about twenty 25 pounder guns lined up in a field firing a salvo, one after the other in quick succession.

At Ypres we would await delivery of new British tanks and train with them in preparation for the advance into Germany. Operations in Holland, by this time, seemed to be static because of the weather and there were still pockets of enemy resistance at Antwerp and the coast. Also, our tanks were worn out and needed replacing.

As we travelled south it was reassuring to see the long, seemingly unending, convoy of tanks and lorries bringing more reinforcements up to the front. When one is the leading troop in battle it can make one feel that one is alone.

Passing through Holland into Belgium, we halted in a large park on the outskirts of Brussels. Here we parked our Shermans and transferred to lorries for the journey to Ypres.

Chapter 6
Ypres and The Ardennes

The little city of Ypres had fortunately been by-passed in the push northwards and suffered no damage. On arrival the population welcomed us into their homes, one or two men to each household. The Cloth Hall, in the centre of the square, became the regimental dining hall and headquarters.

I and another man were welcomed into the home of a Mr and Mrs Vannassche at No 11 Elizabeth Straat, just off the square.

Me with Mr and Mrs Vannassche, 11 Elizabeth Straat, Ypres Belgium, 4 February 1945

They could not speak English, but they had a teenage daughter named Lucienne who could and through whom I communicated. Mr Vannassche enquired about my Christian name. When I told him it was Ernest he said he would not call me that as it was too much like the German Ernst. When I told him my second name was Leslie he smilingly said, 'We'll call you Leslie then'.

Lucienne Vannassche, aged 16
(the back of the photo is inscribed by Lucienne 'to my beautiful brother from his sincerely sister Lucienne, xxx')

A very warm relationship soon grew up between me and this family. They made me feel almost as though I was their son.

One afternoon after arriving home at 11 Elizabeth Straat, after my training session, Mrs Vannassche said 'would you like to go and meet Lucienne from work?' She had a little job at the music shop not far away. I often wondered whether Mr and Mrs Vannassche had once wanted a son as well as a daughter, for they treated me as one of the family. In fact, in a way they became Mum and Dad to me in those days between battles. As Lucienne once said, 'You are my English brother'.

I found the shop 'Steven's Music' two streets away. She seemed surprised to see me and enquired if I would like to buy a record. They were mostly 78rpm I recall. I selected one of Tchaikovsky's Waltz and Polonaise, from his opera Eugene Onegin. She said, 'I will sign it for you as a little souvenir'. I still have that recording signed on the label but I am unable to play it which is disappointing. She also gave me two photographs, one of her mother and father with me, which she took, and one of herself. Perhaps she was attracted to me. I seemed to make few male friends but more friends with girls.

Another day, Lucienne's mother said 'You have your meals with us'. I told her that I had to eat in the army's dining area. 'No, no', she replied, 'You see your officer'. I got his permission, providing I was back at the training classes on the new tanks - which had not actually arrived at that time. Evening meals with the Vannassches were quite an occasion. They could easily last for 2 hours, for we talked a lot as we ate. At breakfast she made lots of pancakes with maple syrup. They were small but she made lots of them and kept serving them to me.

I remember that another soldier sent to their house moved out after the first day. I asked Lucienne why he had gone. All she said was that 'He was not a very nice boy'. I guessed that perhaps he had made advances to her, which is not surprising being as charming as she was. When he had gone, Mrs Vannassche said 'You have a better room now'. I was moved to a larger room downstairs. It was so comfortable after all the rain, mud and cold of Holland. I visited all their friends and later when I was moved to Germany, I often took a weekend's leave to go to Ypres, for just a couple of days and their welcome was always warm and genuine. So the war was not all battles and bullets.

For some weeks as we waited for the new tanks from England, I lived and ate together with the Vannassches, visiting their friends and going to the cinema. 11 Elizabeth Straat became a home from home. Christmas was approaching and in every home preparations were being made to make it a happy one. We looked forward to sharing the season with people who were so warm and hospitable. But it was not to be. The sudden reports that the German army had broken through American forces in the Ardennes region and threatened to drive to Brussels and the coast, came as a nasty jolt to our comfortable situation. In just 30 hours we raced to Brussels to collect our tanks, now vandalised by souvenir hunters, but soon put into battle shape and then moved into positions at Givet.

It was a hard winter in 1944 and the roads to the Ardennes were icy and snowbound, but the Brigade had never moved so fast and we were ready to halt the menacing threat several miles ahead. We arrived in the town of Givet to find it occupied by American troops. They seemed quite unperturbed by the fact that the German divisions had breached our defences near Bastogne and they were in danger. A lorry loaded with black American soldiers passed us at great speed. One of them, wearing a top hat ridiculously perched on this head shouted out to us, 'Man we're getting the hell outa here!' He obviously knew of the critical position further up the front.

We crossed the bridge in the town, over the River Meuse, and were ordered that if the Germans reached Givet, we were to blow the bridge behind us and fight on the opposite bank to the finish. Thankfully we did not have to. We pushed on through the town to engage what enemy troops lay ahead. We moved further south, probing into suspected areas of the country, finally making the little village of Beauraing our base. From there, patrols were sent out daily to check the advance of enemy forces. Intelligence reports came that German parachutists in American uniforms were being dropped, and I and another member of our troop were ordered to watch from the bell tower of the local church.

On Christmas Eve, as we watched, a service was going on below us in the church; the priest ringing little bells in the Communion service. Luckily we did not spot any enemy parachutes. Christmas day 1944, a bitterly cold day, was spent drinking hot strong coffee supplied by the landlord of the local inn, and frozen bully beef sandwiches.

For two weeks we remained on full alert but it appeared that the momentum of the German advance was slowing down. They were probably running out of supplies and it eventually petered out. It was decided that a limited number of crews could have leave in England, the first since we had landed in Normandy and I was fortunate to be in the first group chosen. The regiment remained in the area for another week before returning to Ypres, while fresh troops took over our positions on the front.

Returning to Ypres, we celebrated Christmas and New Year with our Belgian friends. I returned from a week's leave to find that everyone was to have a medical examination in preparation for the next phase in the war, which would be the advance into Germany.

It turned out, however, that several of us proved not to be fit enough. An A1 standard of fitness is required of tank crews and my examination, along with others who had been badly affected by the Holland episode resulted in being downgraded to B1. This meant we could no longer serve in future combat. It was very disappointing having come through so much to have to leave the regiment and the men we had fought alongside.

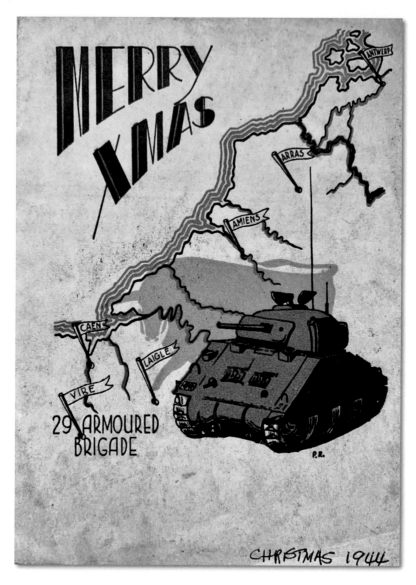

Xmas card, 23rd Hussars 1944, showing the drive to Antwerp

This completes the story of my time in action with the 23rd Hussars, 29th Armoured Brigade, 11th Armoured Division.

Chapter 7
New Postings

I was one of a number of men duly dispatched to a holding unit in Bruges, a not unpleasant posting, for this 'Venice of the North', as it is sometimes called, is a pretty town and I enjoyed my short stay there.

Various artists from the U.K. were in the town to entertain the troops. There was a well-known jazz band whose name I cannot remember and also the music lecturers, Dobson and Young. Back home they used to broadcast music lectures for schools on the wireless, as we referred to radio in those days. Dobson did the talking whilst Young operated the record player. The way they synchronized the lecture and the music was very clever. One piece of music I remember was Vaughan Williams, Overture to the Wasps, in which the buzzing of a wasp is heard in the opening string section. A long descending chord is played to suddenly stop before the entry of a folk song. Dobson anxiously looked all around and as the chord is heard, clasps his neck as though he had been stung. Another piece I remember was the 4th movement of Beethoven's 8th Symphony. In the last bars the music is repeated over and over again. Dobson likened this to an after-dinner speaker who does not know when to shut up and sit down. Dobson and Young worked marvellously together and brought out the humour in music.

During my short stay in Bruges, I was able to wander around the town. I entered one of the churches to find the bible chained to the lectern, and I was reminded how much this book was treasured and guarded in the early years of printing. Every year near Easter there is a procession of the priests and dignitaries, who carry what they believe to be a phial of the blood of Jesus Christ. There is in fact a church known as the Basilica of the Holy Blood.

From Bruges was another move, this time to Brussels, where we billeted in large empty blocks on the outskirts of the city. For about two weeks I had nothing to do but see the sights of the city. We were required only to report every morning while we waited for our final posting. I visited the Theatre de la Monet to see Madame Butterfly, heard a concert on 'The Art of the Fugue by Bach' at the Beaux Arts Concert Hall and after a long search, found the Manneken Pis sculpture, in a tiny corner of a street.

The story behind this rather rude little statue, so we were told, relates to a time long ago when the young son of a notable citizen of the city was lost. Everyone was ordered to search the narrow streets and bring him home safely to the family. A reward was offered and it was agreed that in whatever circumstances the little boy was found, a monument would be erected. To this day the little statue of a small boy urinating in the corner of a street can be seen and it is a tourist attraction. On certain occasions it is dressed up to celebrate his discovery by the frantic parent.

It was a marvellous place to celebrate my 21st birthday. I found the Wesley Church, for Methodism of course is a worldwide denomination, and I remember attending a unique service where we sang alternately hymns in French and English, where I found a feeling of unity with those of a different culture than ours. Another memory I have of Brussels, is the overcrowded trams that operated until the early hours of the morning. They were always full of people desperate to get to their chosen destination, even standing precariously on the running board of the trams. I found Brussels a lively, very busy place to be, even in wartime; for the advance of the allies had long since passed and were now threatening Germany itself. I thought also of my mates of the 23rd Hussars and wondered how they all were.

The posting eventually came and I was driven to Krefeld, a town just inside the German border, to a new unit, the headquarters of the General Headquarters troops (GHQ), which was formed to administer the affairs of the British Army after the cessation of hostilities. It was while I was here that first reports came that an armistice had been signed on Luneburg Heath in North Germany. A day or two later I was with the advance party travelling to Bad Salzuflen, to set up the headquarters, to administer the affairs of all British Forces in Germany.

Headquarters GHQ Troop, Bad Salzuflen Germany January 1946,
Me, front row, second from the right

Bad Salzuflen is one of the major health resorts of Westphalia and boasts some fine buildings and lovely parks. Our headquarters building was the actual Spa town's reception offices, a large imposing building on the edge of the park. We commandeered the Der Quellenhof Hotel which stood opposite. It was a small hotel with about twenty to thirty rooms above a restaurant and wine bar.

In the few days before the main party arrived, we enjoyed the luxury of tablecloths on the meal table and the services of a waiter, who treated us with great respect. This soon changed, however, when the rest of the unit came, but the meals that followed were very pleasant.

Der Quellenhof Hotel, Bad Salzuflen, commandeered as living quarters for the HQ GHQ Troops

At first I was given the job of receptionist in the entrance hall of the HQ. One morning an army captain visited us demanding to know in what room Major 'X' could be found. He whacked his cane importantly on the desk as he spoke. I asked someone who he was. 'Don't you know? That's B H Valentine.' The then well-known Kent and England cricketer.

After this my duties alternated between duplicating and despatch clerk and telephone exchange operator and I soon made new friends. Among these new friends was a German telephone operator who manned (or should I say womaned) the exchange at Walsrode, a town about 10 kilometres away. When on night duty on the HQ telephone we used to chat to pass the hours away. By this time, we were free to fraternise with the German population, something that was not previously allowed. She had a deep sultry voice and I wondered what she looked like. So did other men who took telephone duty. We made a date to meet at 'halb sieben' but she did not turn up. Talking to her the next night she said I was late. I realised then that halb sieben, or half past seven as I understood it to be was really half an hour before seven, in fact half past six. So I never knew what she looked like nor ever met her.

Group in Bad Salzuflen, me, back row second from right
(NB: I was the only one from a tank corps with a black beret)

I became one of a group of five staff who were music fanatics and we took every opportunity to attend symphony concerts, wherever locally they were held. We were fortunate to hear the famous Berlin Philharmonic on various occasions and also went to, what must have been one of the last recitals of Elizabeth Schumann, the celebrated soprano. There were visits by Sadler's Wells Opera and the Glasgow Orpheus Choir under their dedicated conductor, Hugh Robertson. We acquired a portable gramophone and some classical records and regularly held private concerts of our own in each other's rooms.

Kurpark, Bad Salzuflen, Germany, 1945

At Herford, a few miles away, Captain Joe Cooper, an army education officer at the time, also held record concerts. Often playing the solo piano part himself along with the recording. These evenings were attended by 'squaddies' and officers alike. After he returned to civilian life, Joe Cooper appeared often on television, presenting classical music quizzes which quickly gained popularity with many viewers. Altogether the weeks spent at Bad Salzuflen were very happy ones, walking in the large park and in the forest above the town. There were deer running wild in the forest and various paths which had carved signposts along the way decorated with animals. We spent many a pleasant Sunday afternoon walking in the woods and I thought of the children's fairy story of Hansel and Gretel, which of course was made into an opera. We never came across the little cottage made of sweets, which comes into the story.

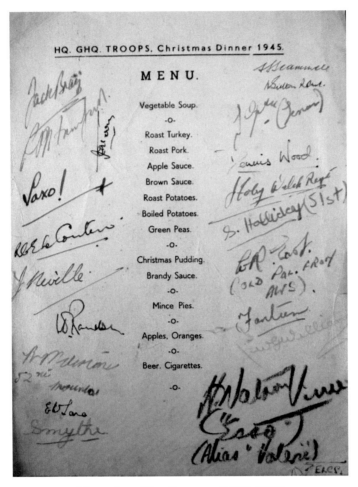

Menu signed by the men of HQ GHQ

There was a large lake in the park on which we took a boat one afternoon. We had to row for our lives when we unwittingly disturbed some swans nesting on a little island. The male bird can be very fierce and protective and swam after us, almost catching up with us as we breathlessly reached the safety of the shore. Never argue with a swan, especially when they are looking after their young cygnets.

In July 1945, I was given 10 days leave and sailed from Cuxhaven to Harwich. Taking the train to London and then from the capital to Gillingham. I found that this train was the last one, so I decided to hitch hike the ten or eleven miles home to Milton. It was a clear summer's night and the smell of honeysuckle from the gardens as I walked the A2, filled the night air.

During the next few days Jean and I often went to the cinema. On one occasion we took the train to London, to spend the day there and I proposed to her as we left Sittingbourne. It was to prove one of the most important moments of my life and the first step to our future together. The date was July 27th. Jean's sister Rhoda gave us an engagement party in her room above a photographer's studio in Station Street, Sittingbourne.

Rhoda and husband Sydney in about 1997

These were relaxing days in Bad Salzuflen and later in life I often wished I could return to this beautiful part of Westphalia.

Soon we were sending out orders for groups of men due for demob and eventually there was no need for as many staff, so I found myself stationed about 100 miles further Northeast. I was posted to No 3 Civilian Internment Camp (No 3 CIC) situated on high ground about a mile out of Fallingbostel. The camp enclosure housed about two hundred German civilians, of all professions, who were suspected of collaboration with the Nazi regime. About forty British personnel were in charge of the administration and the perimeter guard duties fell to the Polish unit. My job was in the orderly room, which was situated at the main gate of the camp. At weekends, relatives of the inmates were allowed to visit and they had to report here, before going under escort into the prison compound. Many of the prisoners were craftsmen and made objects out of waste materials of wood and leather etc. I had a workbox made, which I parcelled up and sent home. I still use this workbox. Also, I have a leather wallet bearing the coat of arms of Fallingbostel. It is rather crude and heavy but it shows how some of these men spent their time in custody. One particular prisoner, who had been to Scotland and then transferred there had studied the poems of Robert Burns. He could recite many of them.

Living in wooden huts, exposed to the weather, it was a far cry from the comfort of Bad Salzuflen. This was to be my last move in the services and I made the best of it. There was a Toc H[11] club in the village and I became friendly with the warden and staff. Harry Ashton, The Toc H club warden took a particular interest in me. I think he was a Methodist preacher because when I told him I had just begun to start my studies for a local preacher he immediately

---

[11] Toc H is an abbreviation for Talbot House, a rest and recreational centre for troops, originating from the 1st World War.

said, 'Well you can do them here by correspondence course. I can arrange that for you and provide a tutor.

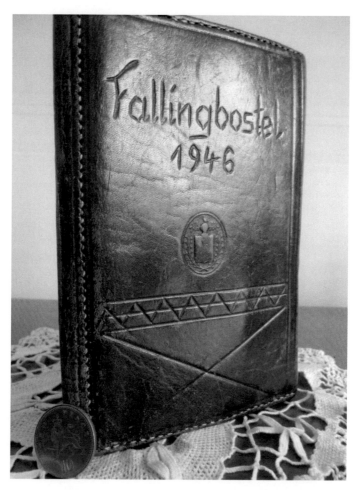

Leather Wallet made by a prisoner in Fallingbostel

Needlework Box from No 3 CIC, Fallingbostel

You will give me the answers to the questions after each stage of the course to post on to London Methodist Central Hall and the tutor will send you his response and advice.' So I agreed to take the Old Testament course which would take about twelve months. The tutor, whose name I do not remember, lived in Kings Lynn. Sometimes he would write back 'You could have enlarged your answers', which I then did. Then on another occasion he wrote 'Well you could have answered the set questions in fewer words'. This annoyed me a little, but I was determined to carry on studying the set syllabus. It was not easy with other duties, but I completed it. Harry invited me to share in running the weekly services and I got to know the staff who were all German residents at Fallingbostel. We had discussions at Toc H about getting Germany back on its feet again and the reinstatement of local government. It was interesting to be part of all this while in No3 CIC.

A few weeks later, I learned of the 23rd Hussars discovery of the notorious concentration camp at Belsen about six kilometres away.

It was a chilling reminder of the barbarity of the Nazis. The villagers said they knew nothing of its existence. I think they probably did for the smell of decaying bodies hung in the air when the wind was in our direction. Perhaps they had been sworn to secrecy, or were afraid of admitting their knowledge. I learned also that on the advance of the 23rd Hussars towards Hamburg, they must have passed this way for they were met with a warning sign which said 'Achtung Typhus'. Sometime later the regiment arrived at their last camp, a modern German barracks at Husum in Schleswig Holstein, where the 11th Armoured Division and the 23rd were disbanded.

I began my studies to become a local preacher. It had been four years since I was forced by the war to suspend them. So I took up a correspondence course with my tutor in Kings Lynn, Norfolk. It went very well and after a few months I was ready to take the exam on the Old Testament part of the course. The Toc H warden happened to be a Christian, though I don't remember which denomination. Anyway he made the Reading Room available for me to sit the exam. The result duly arrived and I was pleased to hear that I had passed at sixty five percent, the pass mark being 60%.

Back at camp, men began to receive their demob papers. The staff was reduced to twenty of us. Because we were all doing the bulk of the work the CO decided to promote some of us to the rank of Sergeant. I received my stripes with all the privileges that went with it, except increased pay. It was a local, acting promotion, but as it would not be long before my release came, I did not mind.

We had a very crafty SQMS (Squadron Quartermasters Sergeant) who still indented for forty men's rations, so our food was very good indeed and I put on so much weight. Our SQMS could be nasty sometimes, so one night after he had been to the village, got drunk and gone to bed, two of my mates got their own back. They carried him, still fast asleep and out for the count, outside the hut, sticking a little fir tree that they had dug up from somewhere, under the blanket with him.

Fallingbostel No 3, Civil Internment Camp, N Germany, 1946

They were not to know that weather would change, but it poured hard all night and the poor chap woke up thoroughly drenched. He had no clue who had done this cowardly act. In spite of a bit of a cold he treated it all as a joke.

In the early part of 1947, I was due for leave and the winter that year was particularly harsh. On returning to Cuxhaven the ship had to cut its way into port, the sea for many yards being covered with ice. The journey across Holland and Germany was a horrendous one, six-foot drifts of snow covered a large area. In our wooden huts it was freezing cold and the heating was just an old tortoise stove in the centre of the building. We would wake up to find our shirts frozen stiff. We must have been very fit in those days for the weather did not bother us much and life went on as usual. One day the CO said that men were wanted to join Control Commission for Germany. This was an organisation to set up local governments again. The pay was attractive, accommodation would be available with a uniform, car and a German house servant. It certainly looked inviting. However, I had recently received letters from Jean, my Fiancée back in England, wanting me to name a date for the wedding. Ruby, a lifelong school friend of hers had a house and would be willing to let us have two rooms. I thought about the job a lot and, after I had told my mates about the letter, they said that I should accept it.

Although the Control Commission offer was attractive, I had had enough of the army and wanted to get home. The thought of getting married on demob excited me, so the date was fixed for May 31st. On April 7th I left Germany for the last time and arrived in Harwich, from where I took the train to York. Here I shed my army uniform and collected a dark pinstripe suit etc. and a warrant for three months leave plus £80 gratuity.

It seemed a lot of money, but it really was not much to start back into civilian life again. There was still rationing and furniture and blankets etc. were only obtainable with dockets. At least the war was over and I was back home ready to pick up the threads of life once again. My army career was over and there was the expectation of a new married life with Jean, a teenage sweetheart.

Jean in the Land Army Uniform, 1946

This lovely photograph of Jean in 1946 speaks so much of her caring personality and love, and I treasure it, and look at it often.

Chapter 8
Marriage

Wedding, May 31st 1947, Milton Chapel

The reader may become aware that I am gleaning events in my life from diaries. I have kept a diary since 1946 and have found them particularly useful in compiling the sequence of events of my life.

As a civilian once again, I prepared to take up life where my army career ended and that great change began with my marriage to Jean. It meant at first coming home and planning for that important day.

For the time being anyway, I made a home with my grandparents and Jean and I began planning for the big day. The winter of 1946/47 resulted in a great deal of flooding in low-lying areas but it was followed by a very hot May. Tar bubbled up in the roads on the 31st and it was a hot humid day. Jean and I were married in the little Methodist Chapel in Milton, in the town in which we had both grown up. The wedding caused much interest and workmen of the Paper Mill surveyed the scene from the high wall opposite the church. It was also reported well in the local newspaper and occupied half a page.

The reception was held in the Sittingbourne Methodist School Hall and afterwards we took the train to Bridlington for our week's honeymoon. I had suggested Yorkshire because I had enjoyed a happy few months there during the war. In June, however, Bridlington is not very warm. East winds keep the atmosphere quite cool but we enjoyed the stay in the seaside town, visiting several old friends I had known so well during my army service there. At the guesthouse where we stayed, we unpacked our suitcase to find it full of confetti which spilled all over the bedroom floor. Someone somehow had managed to open our luggage. We apologised to the proprietors who only laughed and thought it quite a joke. We never found out who did this.

Honeymoon in Bridlington

One day, being a keen gramophone record collector, I bought a record of the celebrated Italian tenor, Beniamino Gigli. Coming out of the shop we met some friends I knew. 'What is the music on your record?' 'I'll walk beside you', we told them. 'And what is on the other side?' I had not actually looked but turning the disc over noticed that the title was 'Parted' by Tosti. Was it a bad omen? I don't think so for we stayed together for over 60 years, until Jean sadly died. The reason for buying the record was that Jean would always hold my hand when we went out walking.

Back home again, we began our life together, buying the essential furniture we needed. One could not purchase a great deal at that time. It was just not available so soon after the war, but we got together the basic things to make a home.

The house in Crown Road, Milton Regis was not far from where I was born. It was a more modern building, and Jean and I shared the house with Ruby. Ruby Willmore was an old friend of Jean's, as I have already mentioned and we had the use of the back rooms of the house with the little necessary furniture that we were able to buy, plus some cork lino floor covering which was all the fashion in those days. Ruby's husband Fred was away doing his national service. I began working again at Bobbing Court Farm. I had always liked the outdoor life, and though the wages were not good enough, I enjoyed the work, particularly having a liking for picking fruit and moving ladders. Ladder handling, I found is an art and I soon mastered it and felt grand to look across the countryside from the top of a sixty-foot ladder. Fruit orchards like this have completely disappeared from the Kent rural scene. Now trees are only 6 ft high and can easily be picked from a stepladder.

The next four years were to be one of turmoil for me and Jean. We could not get a home of our own, in spite of frequent visits to the offices of the council. Servicemen were promised houses when the war was over and we were shown prefabricated temporary dwellings that would be available. But we and many others were bitterly disappointed.

After a while we moved from Crown Road to Jean's Grandfather's house in Chestnut Street, just off the Maidstone Road. Things did not work out well at first, for Granddad did not like us to be out after 9pm. One night we missed the bus and arrived home late, so we got a bad reception.

Grandmother Taylor who gave me a home after Mother's death in 1937

So we moved then to Jean's old home at 4 Kingsmill Road, where her mother gave us a room. It was a bit crowded though because other members of Jean's family lived there. My Grandmother who had brought me up when my mother died said we could live with her at Milbourne Grove, but when it was discovered that Jean was to have a baby, my grandfather told us we must move. So it happened that we returned to Kingsmill Road once more. I have often said that our home in those days was on the back of a lorry more often than in a house.

I continued my preaching course once again. I had passed the first Old Testament exam in Fallingbostel. Now it was the second stage, studies on the New Testament. Jean was an officer in the Girls Life Brigade and attended her meetings at our East Street church on Monday evenings. (This building is now a sports centre) We would walk into town together. I would leave Jean at the church whilst I would go on to the minister's manse, a hundred yards away. Reverend Vincent Jay, my tutor, was a slightly built, rather frail man but an excellent teacher.

I took up training appointments once again and the day came for me to take my final oral exam. This oral test, at the Superintendent's manse in Park Road, was quite an ordeal. Present were the two ministers, and all the serving experienced preachers of the circuit. As a new recruit I was questioned thoroughly, I might add mercilessly, for half an hour, on my knowledge of the Bible and theology in general. I was then sent out of the room whilst the meeting discussed my suitability as a potential preacher. I returned, what seemed an age later, to be told that I had been accepted on condition I passed the trial service, to be conducted in the presence of two ministers. This I was able to do to the satisfaction of my tutor. However, this is not the final stage in a preacher's training. A recommendation has to go to the church council which usually is just a formality. After that a public recognition service of my status as a fully accredited Methodist local preacher was arranged. It is a lengthy process but I felt very pleased that I had managed to complete my training. Once authorised, a man or woman (for we have lady preachers in Methodism, as well) is allowed to conduct worship in other places in the United Kingdom, if and when such an invitation is received. A Methodist local preacher receives no payment. It is purely a voluntary service given and brings its own rewards. So slowly I got back into the routine of civvy street, making a life together with Jean and ready to face the world together.

To return to my work, the wages were poor at Bobbing Court, although I enjoyed the work but it was not enough, so I took a job at the Kemsley Paper Mill with the help of Mr Witts. I joined what was known as the yard gang. This was a pool of labourers who could be called on to do a variety of tasks or replace anyone who went absent. I worked on the log floor, also the place where the reel centres are cut, and on the super calendar machines which put the final gloss on to the finished newsprint, etc. I also helped packing the reels of paper when they had been produced. I found it hard and demoralising at times, having to work inside.

It was at 4 Kingsmill Road that our first child was born. I happened to be on night shift at the mill and was preparing to go to work when Jean started labour. Anxiously I rushed to Staplehurst Road where the nurse, Mrs Marshall lived and she came to attend her. I decided that the arrival of the baby was too imminent to go to work that night and being the first child, I was worried for Jean. The baby was eventually born at 11.15 the next morning and delivered by a student nurse under supervision. I think she passed the test. It was a girl just as we had dreamed of. What would we name her?

There was at that time a comedy show on the radio called 'Itma'[12] with Tommy Handley as the leading character. One of the features of the show was the unexpected interruption to the programme by various people wandering onto the set. One favourite was a little girl who wandered innocently into the studio and Tommy asked her 'What is your name' and she replies 'My name is Jennifer' in a shy nervous voice. So, Jennifer it had to be.

---

[12] Itma is an abbreviation for 'It's that man again'.

On the night Jean was in labour and expecting our first child, my Grandfather came home on the bus, crossed the road afterwards and walked into an oncoming car. He was killed instantly. I thought how strange things happen sometimes. One life taken and a new one is born. Because he had not wanted us, as Jean was expecting a baby, I thought, fate had played a cruel trick on him. It seemed to be that way but I am sure now, that it was just a tragic coincidence. But for this accident he could have lived to see our first child, and I know he would have accepted the addition to the family with as much joy as Jean and I did.

It was also at Kingsmill Road that I arrived home from work early one morning to find the streets of Milton flooded. During the spring tides it was not unusual that the creek overflowed its banks and drains would fill up everywhere. It caused much damage and misery to those living near the head of the creek and took months to make homes habitable again. Sometimes homes were flooded to a depth of 3 feet, so one can imagine the distress it caused.

Chapter 9
Life After the War

It is difficult to briefly summarise life after the war, looking back at the age of 97, over those 73 years since leaving the army and returning from Germany in 1947 to get married. But I will try.

As mentioned in Chapter 8, Jean and I started our married life in Milton Regis near Sittingbourne in Kent, where our first child Jennifer was born in 1949. In 1951 we moved to Newington, a village nearby, where I worked for Swale Rural District Council as storekeeper, and later as buyer. Our house in Church Lane was one of two old semi-detached Victorian buildings, in need of some repair. However, we were so thrilled that at last we had a home of our own, after living in rooms with friends and relatives for 4 years. I remember on entering the house for the first time, having to negotiate an old harp which stood just inside the front door of the room. Its strings were broken and hanging on the floor and it made a peculiar twanging noise as I brushed past it. I noticed too, as I came in, bottles and piles of old newspapers covering the sides of the stairs. It was owned by two old ladies who I learned were members of a Spiritualist Church in Gillingham and they said they believed we had been 'sent'. We were told that we could have the house at a low rent, if we could do any minor repairs ourselves.

Being from the town, we were not readily accepted by some of the neighbours initially and they peered through their curtains at these new arrivals in the road. However, we soon made ourselves known and made many friends.

This was the beginning of almost 30 years as members of a village community, with many happy experiences. Before moving to Swale Borough Council, I worked at Kemsley Paper Mill and made friends with Joe Denne who was a steward of Newington Methodist church. We cycled home from work together many times. One night it was very foggy, so bad was it that we had extreme difficulty in seeing the road before us. Near Bobbing village we heard the sound of an animal and out of the gloom a cow, that had strayed from the meadow, appeared like a spectre from another world. But no harm came to us, nor the spectre from another world.

We had not got a lot of money in those days and often Jean would travel on the bus to Milton chapel, where we still worshipped, taking Jennifer with her. I would cycle there and meet her. On one occasion I thought it would be a good idea to take Jennifer home on my bike. I literally carried her in the crook of my arm, cycling with one hand, the three miles home to Newington. Jennifer, aged 2, thought it was lovely, looking all around as we travelled home. My arm was ready to drop off when we reached Church Lane where we lived. I often think of this and how I must have been mad to even think of doing such a crazy thing. Even though the traffic was light compared to today.

My son David was born in 1952. He was a bonny fair-headed little boy and we had problems with Jennifer, now about 2 years old. I believe she was jealous of him at first and cried continuously for a week or so, and we were very worried for a while, but eventually she accepted her little brother. We now had a little family and we both felt very proud and fortunate to have a boy and a girl. We watched them grow up from the time they first walked, when Jennifer strayed into the backyard and started chewing coke from the bucket outside the back door, to the day they started school at Newington. I have always felt that some of the hardest, though happiest days in parents' lives are those when children are very young before they go to school.

The year of 1956 proved to be a turning point in our lives and I felt very lucky to have secured work at Swale Rural District Council in Newington, not far from home. On my first day, a Monday morning, I arrived at the Council depot which was situated in a valley on the road to Lower Halstow. It consisted of a huddle of buildings, the main stores being once the concrete shelter used during the war. It was a dull wet miserable day and I thought that I had jumped out of the frying pan into the fire, so dismal was the scene. The surveyor told me that a new store was planned for the future but would not be built for a while. So I had to make the best of things, warming myself in the 'office' by an old-fashioned tortoise stove which sent out coke fumes. Meanwhile events progressed at home. John, Jean's youngest brother, did the basic electric wiring of the house in Church Lane. It had gas lighting when we moved in. I did a lot of decorating to brighten up what had been a rather drab place.

I cultivated the little garden, planting new potatoes in neat rows which I later earthed up and over which Jennifer and David drove relentlessly with their tricycles. I did leave a little plot for them to sow seeds for themselves. After sowing them Jennifer would go down to the plot every day to see if they had grown.

With the encouragement of Jean we bought our first radiogram. Before this I had a small Dansette record player on which to play my records, the number of which was increasing. The new gramophone was shaped like a coffin on legs but had a lovely sound and the children loved to dance round the room to the sounds of the Toreador's song from Bizet's Carmen. I am certain that, were it not for Jean, I would never have bought anything more modern. I was previously quite happy with my wind-up Colombia portable machine which only played 78s.

One of the wartime concrete sheds at the depot in Newington served as the carpenters' shop. One morning one of the joiners went into an outbuilding where an old air raid siren was stored. It was still in good working order, which he found out to his cost. For some unknown reason other than sheer curiosity, he put his finger into one of the openings. The siren propeller was well oiled for it turned causing his finger to be nearly severed at the first joint. He came running into the workshop, laughing and pointing at his damaged finger, the top of which had almost been severed. He felt nothing but numbness for a minute or so, but when it came to, he was in terrible pain. Someone quickly got him to a doctor and he was very lucky to have it sewn back and it eventually healed.

Both of the children loved books. Jennifer's favourites were the Noddy series of children's stories, which were very popular at that time. This character, with his pointed hat with the little bell on the top, was a great favourite. David's hero was Rupert Bear. The Rupert stories seem to go on forever and we tried to close the book, saying that was the last one, but you couldn't fool him. Long past his bedtime he would say, 'One more story, Daddy.' And he usually got his way. We had always felt it important to read to our children and I am sure they have learned a great deal from books.

I continued to make small improvements to the house and later in the year we had a new deep sink fitted in the kitchen after removing the old copper which had been built in a corner of the room. We wished that we had a bathroom. We had to use a galvanised bath which hung outside on the wall and was brought into the kitchen to take a bath. This could be embarrassing. One evening when I had settled myself down for a welcome soak, a friend, Mrs Cudmore knocked on the back door. I was on my own so could not get to see her. Instead I had to hold a conversation with her through the closed door. I often think about this incident with amusement, although I was not all that comfortable at the time.

Things were beginning to happen with regard to the future of our little chapel in Milton. I was appointed Trustee's secretary and attended several meetings to discuss this important issue. As much as we were opposed to it, it seemed inevitable that worship would cease. Services were discontinued but a Sunday School afternoon session went on for a while. The day came however, when the final service was held. Gordon Witts, who had spent most of his life with the young people there, could not hide his feelings and was almost in tears. We all felt very sad to have to say goodbye to a place that had so many happy memories for us, and the care by the leaders of that Sunday School that had done much to shape our lives. It was another milestone in our lives and we felt it difficult to accept at the time. As Trust secretary, it was my job to make an inventory of all the contents and see that they were distributed to other churches who might need them. As members, we were able to buy some little memento. I chose to purchase an electric fire and a piano stool. I could not have obtained a more appropriate memento of Milton than the stool, for it reminds me of all the pianists who used it for the various services and school sessions. Their names flash through my mind as I see it. There have been the various jokes about it. At least one young lady believes that by sitting on it she became pregnant. My son David, now in his 60s, vows it was the cause of Philip, their son coming into the world, when they lived with us in Sittingbourne for a time after returning from Saudi Arabia. As I said, the closing and eventual demolition of Milton Chapel marked the end of a chapter.

I realised much later that perhaps I was too much concerned with matters of the church and neglected my family because of it. However, in later years I tried to make up for it, and Jean and I realised that the church had played a great and fulfilling part in our lives which gave us a sense of true values. Also our Methodist upbringing led us to many good and lasting friendships.

The Swale Rural District Council depot was situated in a valley and just outside the boundary fence, a channel fed into the creek two miles away, at Lower Halstow. Just a few yards from this boundary fence there were a number of deep wells, one of which was over 300ft deep. Water from underground springs fed the channel which produced good quality watercress. Once a week, on Friday I used to order bunches for the men in the depot, freshly cut to order. We paid 1 shilling (5 pence in money today) for about half a pound of cress. I am not sure the springs are there any longer.

Working for the Swale Rural District Council was one of the happiest times in my life, for there was a spirit of friendly co-operation between workmen and office staff, which I found woefully missing later. We became so busy at Newington, as time went by, that I was given an assistant to help me in the stores. Bob was a strange mixture. He could be very helpful and friendly but also aggressive in his attitude, at other times. He knew I was involved with the church and he lost no time in ridiculing the church and used to say that vicars only worked one day a week. In spite of these taunts we got along fairly well and he had a kind side to his nature.

So life at work went on smoothly and happily. During the season I did a lot of fruit picking to earn a little extra and Jean worked in various homes doing housework and looking after children in Hartlip, a village a mile away.

In January 1963 we received a letter from the council to say we had been allocated one of the new council houses being built in Playstool Close, Newington, not far away from our house in Church Lane. Jean was so excited about the prospect of us moving into a brand-new home and could hardly wait for the builders to complete the site.

The first thing Jean wanted to do, as soon as we had moved in, was to have a bath in a proper bathroom that had hot running water. To her it was sheer luxury. Thinking about it all now makes me feel how much we take for granted the various facilities of a modern home. Starting as we and many others of our age did, with almost nothing, we can truly appreciate these things. So, for the first time, we were happily installed in a new house.

Our association with Edward and Penelope Lyndon-Stanford was one of the highlights of our years in Newington. They lived in an old Queen Anne house in Church Lane just a few yards from where we had lived. The house known as 'Hollybank' was situated on high ground above the road and featured an unusual wrought iron fence. This was fixed to the top of the wall in the front of the property and consisted of an interesting leaf design.

Hollybank House

The property bordered the main railway from London to Dover. At the rear of the house were extensive lawns and a small cherry orchard. Within the boundary also there was a cottage which the Lyndon-Stanford's rented out. This and the house were reached by a steep drive to the left of the house. There were two garages which housed veteran Rolls Royce limousines, one of the various hobbies of Edward. A side entrance led into two kitchens, the floors of which were made up of large York stone slabs, a feature which Penelope particularly loved.

To the left of the front entrance was the lounge and across the hall to the right a large dining room. A winding staircase led up to the first floor. At the front of the house were two main bedrooms one of which had a four-poster bed, the other being the guest bedroom.

Mr Stanford was a collector of old clocks and a variety of these were in the couple's bedroom. On one occasion while they were away, we stayed at the house to look after the children - at that time, two girls named Catherine and Emma. The clocks, chiming at different hours of the night, kept us awake.

The house still stands as it was when Jean and I knew it, an interesting house with a great deal of character.

Mrs Stanford at the time we began to visit Hollybank was looking for someone to help in the house. So it happened that Jean went to see her and consequently took the job. As Jean loves children, it was not long before she began taking an interest in the girls and quite a happy relationship took place with the family.

Edward was a partner in a patents firm, whose offices were in Lincoln's Inn Fields in London and he would often be seen rushing for the train in the morning.

I was asked if I could assist in the large garden keeping lawns cut and during the season, picking the cherries. Edward could not use a ladder and I was glad to earn a little extra cash. Also, I was never happier than when picking fruit from the top of a ladder and surveying the countryside from such an elevated position. The fruit would be sent up to a London market every day and was of a very good quality.

Edward had musical interests as well as those already mentioned. He was a member of the London Choral Society, who used to perform music as it was originally written. For example, the choir would annually perform Handel's Messiah, set for a small choir and chamber orchestra. He took me, on one occasion, to the Festival Hall for such a performance and I found it so different from the large-scale performances that I was used to hearing. The conductor, John Tobin, was quite an authority on Handel's works and had written several books on the subject. The choir also performed modern music and, on another occasion, I was invited to a performance of the War Requiem, by Benjamin Britten which I found a very moving experience.

We continued to work for the Lyndon-Stanford's in the house and the garden, sharing also in the special family events which came around from time to time. I believe they valued our friendships as much we did theirs.

In May of 1997 Jean and I were to celebrate 50 years of marriage. Preparations for this great event began quite early in the year, many about which I knew little. I had pondered over the question of what kind of gift I could offer Jean on such an occasion. We both felt at a loss to think of anything that we needed. The fact that we could celebrate our 50th was enough itself.

I remembered that I had broken a valued record of Gigli singing the ballad 'I'll walk beside you', which I had purchased while on our honeymoon in Bridlington, Yorkshire in 1947. So I wrote to the BBC in the hope that they had the recording in their archives. Unfortunately, they hadn't, but I was sent a long list of suppliers of old records where I might obtain it. Some were in London, others elsewhere in various towns up and down the country. I thought it would be a good idea to go to London and search these suppliers.

Near Waterloo Station I found a shop which stocked thousands of old recordings. After an hour's search, I came away disappointed. Then I arranged with my granddaughter Rebecca to travel with me to London again to visit two or three other addresses I had been given. The first happened to be completely vacated. Another was also unsuccessful. Finally, in a shop just off Charing Cross Road we enquired for the particular recording. I was told that they would look for it, and they also directed us to another store in a basement of an office a street away. In dusty shelves we saw thousands of 78rpm records, dating back to the 1930s still in their original covers. 'I'll leave you to yourselves' the man said and left. We hunted the shelves without finding what we wanted and we could have easily spent a week looking at all the rows and rows of discs stored. Suddenly, as Rebecca and I were about to give up and leave, the little man appeared again. 'I've got it,' he said. He produced a long-playing disc of many of Benjamin Gigli ballads; among them 'I'll walk beside you' which had been transferred from the 78rpm records to the LPs. I was overjoyed. Our patience had been rewarded and I came home quite thrilled in having tracked it down.

The day of our anniversary came, and Jennifer had arranged a party to which all our friends and family were invited. I produced my gift of Gigli to Jean, now resurrected from history. Another great surprise was a beautiful engraved glass bowl from Jennifer and son-in-law Keith. Keith had engraved the music of I'll walk beside you around the bowl with images of a couple facing a sunset. Also engraved on it was the star sign of the Plough. The significance of this was that when I was posted to Catterick in 1942, I told Jean to look up into the sky at the stars of the Plough when she felt lonely and I would be looking at them as well. I thought this was a very romantic and fitting touch and Jean and I were both thrilled with it.

In 1974 following reorganisation of local council services, my job moved to Sittingbourne, and in due course we moved house back to Sittingbourne. Sometime later at the age of 58, I was made redundant and worked at Freshbake a local frozen food manufacturer for the last 6 years of my working life.

In 2003, at the age of 80, I decided to retire as a Methodist lay preacher, after serving fifty-five years.

Sittingbourne Methodist Chapel 2002

My wife Jean died tragically at the age of 87 in July 2011 following a stroke. Whilst Jean's loss remains a source of sadness, I feel very grateful for the 64 years we spent together - we had a great deal to be thankful for, and had celebrated our diamond anniversary in 2007. I have a growing family including five grandchildren and six great grandchildren, of which I am very proud. Not forgetting my wonderful son and daughter.

With Jean in 2010

In 2016 my daughter Jennifer, at the age of 68 was diagnosed with a brain tumour. She died in 2017 after a long and brave battle with cancer. I miss her dearly, but I am very proud of the way she retained her sense of humour, trying to make light of her condition to the end, in an attempt to avoid her family becoming too upset

Jennifer ran the London Marathon three times, raising almost £5,000 for four charities, namely Action for Children, (previously the National Childrens Home), Kent Air Ambulance, OCD (Obsessive Compulsive Disorder), and Wateraid. Jennifer was a member of the Choir at Sittingbourne Methodist Church and on the day of the first marathon, 16th April 2000, they had a concert together with the Coop Choir, which started at 6.30pm. To the surprise of the rest of the choir she travelled back from London and managed to join them, a few minutes after the start of the concert.

I am very much indebted to Jennifer's husband, my son-in-law Keith, who to this day looks after me, as I live alone in a bungalow nearby.

I have been fortunate to have remained fairly fit into my nineties and my strong connections to the Methodist Church have continued. Having 'retired' as a local preacher in 2003, I continued taking occasional services until 2018, when I held my final retirement service after 70 years.

The service was a wonderful occasion, if not a little embarrassing, listening to the warm words of thanks and congratulations.

Jennifer in her third London Marathon on 17th April 2011

With thankfulness to God

for **dedicated service** in the kingdom of God and
the Church of Christ, as a **Local Preacher** in the
Methodist Church,

this certificate is presented to

Ernest Slarks

admitted as a **Local Preacher**

in the year _____ *1948*

*"For what we preach is not ourselves,
but Jesus Christ as Lord"* 2 Corinthians 4:5

President of the Methodist Conference

Vice-President of the Methodist Conference

27ᵗʰ May 2018

Date

The **Methodist** Church

Methodist Church Long Service Certificate

With Bill Prince at the end of my Retirement Service

With my Grandson Philip, and Great Grandson Aaron at My Retirement Service in 2018

It was not until the 1990's that I started to recall the war years. Many thousands of men had come back from the war like me and had rebuilt their lives and I suppose none of us wanted to speak about our experiences. It was more important to get on with our lives and forget. However, my grandson Philip, born in 1984, started asking me about my time in the war when he was about ten years old. He was very interested and perhaps this is why, in the years that followed I started to write my autobiography. This was entitled 'One Step at A Time' and had thirty chapters and about 80,000 words spanning my childhood through to the year 2000. The first edition was typed up by my son David and his wife Carole and a handful of paperback copies were made. David printed these at home and had them bound by Reading University binding department. These were primarily for the Grandchildren. The book was not formally published.

In the following years I continued to write and David prepared a second edition with new chapters and many photographs embedded in the text. Three copies were produced in hard bound covers in 2003. Much of this book has been produced from material extracted from the second edition of 'One Step at a Time', but additional detail has been added and later years are covered, up to my 97th birthday in March 2020.

The reader will be aware that the church has had a great influence on me. Without its teaching and a strong faith, life for me would have been very different. Such a faith demands actions, and one example is our lunch club at Sittingbourne Methodist Church. Volunteers provide a wholesome meal every Thursday, at a meagre price, and, for those who live alone like me, a friend to talk to. This is the church in action, and we should be proud of the work they do.

Lunch club volunteers, Sittingbourne Methodist Church

Chapter 10
Return to Normandy

I had always felt a longing to return to Normandy, especially to go back to Ypres, where the people of the city made me so welcome. I told my family of this but never believed anything would come of it. They must have thought a great deal about my feelings, for to my surprise in April 1992, they planned to take me back to France and Belgium.

We hired an eight-seater dormobile and on Friday 10th April we set off to Dover for the ferry crossing to Calais. In the party were Jean and I, our children David and Jennifer and Jennifer's husband Keith with their children Rebecca, Robert and Rachel.

From Calais we drove the 240 miles to Caen, where we booked into the Friendly Hotel on the outskirts of the city centre to stay for two nights. In the evening we took a stroll around the city. I tried to imagine how it was in 1944, as I stood by my tank above the city as a merciless barrage of artillery fire rained down on its ancient buildings. Today, it was a beautiful city again, with wide streets and fine buildings.

We found a place for our evening meal in a crowded French restaurant. Early the next morning, after breakfast, we set off for Arromanches and 'Gold Beach', as it had been code-named in 1944. On route we stopped for a while in the village of Cruelly where, in a meadow at the back of the village, in 1944, my regiment had harboured that first night in France. I stood in the square with Jean and David and tried to imagine how it had been that warm dusty June.

When we arrived in Arromanches we found that a dense fog covered the beach and we were unable to see the remains of the

Mulberry harbour, which was constructed to unload military supplies. On the promenade a museum has been built, where we saw a small-scale layout of the invasion of Normandy. Outside stood a 25-pounder gun and a few yards up the road a Sherman tank was parked; reminders of the war.

After a walk around the town, we continued on our journey to Bayeux, to visit the war graves cemetery. Bayeux had been bypassed in the war and had suffered no damage. The cathedral of Notre-Dame, which dominates the town, dates back to the 12th century. It was built on the site of a Roman temple. The bells of the tower rang out across the square, as we walked through the streets.

Arriving later at the gates of the military cemetery, we stopped for a coffee. I had been told by a visitor in Arromanches, a soldier of the Green Howards, who landed on D-Day, that there were some graves here of men of the 23rd Hussars. For some time I wandered around the great burial grounds, with its hundreds of white stones. At last I found the memorials to some of the men I had fought with in 1944, one from my own squadron. To me it was a very moving experience. Here were men who had not survived the battles of Normandy, but I had.

Across the road was the Bayeux War Museum and at the entrance I stood by a Sherman tank for a photograph, another grim reminder of those far off days.

From Bayeux we drove through the Normandy Bocage countryside to Le Beny-Bocage. It was from here, in 1944, we were called to the front. The Regiment was defending a hill above the village of Le Bas Perrier and had suffered many losses. Driving along the narrow lanes I saw the hill, now covered with grass to the left of the road. Through Presles to Chenedolle the memories flooded back to a week when I really felt that I would not come out of this terrifying experience alive.

Next to a Mark IV Sherman tank at Bayeux War Museum - April 1992

The next morning, we packed and made ready for the next stage of our tour, to visit Ypres. Before we left, we decided to visit the Caen Memorial. This is a great limestone cubelike building north of the city. It houses many relics and artefacts of the D-Day landings, with powerful exhibitions of the actual scenes. In a visitors' book I wrote '48 years ago I came in war, today I come in peace'. Nearby is the Nobel Prize Gallery, built over the site of a former German military command post.

We returned to our van to find it had been broken into and Jennifer, Keith and the children's clothes stolen. It was a terrible shock to us and I was so upset that I wanted to abandon the tour. Jennifer undaunted said, 'No it is not going to spoil our tour'. I thought that under the circumstances this was a very brave thing to say. Keith reported the matter to the police and later than we had planned, we set off for Ypres.

After a brief stop at Amiens for a meal, we arrived in Ypres later that evening, booking in at the Hotel Ariene. It was good to be back in the little city, which had been a home for a time in the winter of 1944.

We found our rooms, unpacked and later went along to see Jennifer and the family. Because they had lost all their belongings, they had to clean their teeth with toothpaste borrowed from David and smeared on the face cloths. As they had no nightwear, they had to borrow that as well. Rachel wore my pyjama top much to her amusement, while Rebecca wore one of Jean's nightdresses. They all bravely made a great joke of it all.

The following morning I set out to go to No 11 Elizabeth Straat, where I had found a home with the Vannassche family, after the Holland Campaign. It was just as I had imagined. In fact Ypres was still the same as I knew it years before. The same cobbled streets and friendly atmosphere about the whole town.

Later in Jennifer's room, Jennifer said to Jean 'Shall we tell him?' I only discovered then that she and Keith had written to the Belgian embassy and the Burgomaster of Ypres enquiring after the Vannassches. After a couple of letters and several weeks, they found the new address of Lucienne. Jennifer then wrote to her, but received no reply. David then suggested she had one last try, and to write again stating that we would be in Antwerp on a particular day, and would be at the Villa Mozart Hotel at 12 noon. There was still no reply, so Jennifer did not know whether the letter had been received, let alone whether Lucienne would be willing to meet me.

I was really dumbfounded to hear this - I could not believe there was a slim chance I might meet Lucienne after 48 years.

Not knowing whether the trip would be a waste of time, we were soon on our way to Antwerp. We arrived in pouring rain and parked the van alongside the River Scheldt. We then walked through the cobbled streets to the cathedral square. The clock on the tower said 11.50am. Across the square we came to the Villa Mozart Hotel, where Jennifer had stated in the letter that we would be at noon that day. David went into the hotel and spoke to reception, returning with great excitement to say that Lucienne had called the hotel, asking if we were staying there. At long last after many weeks of writing letters, we knew that Lucienne had received at least the final one. However, we still did not know if she would come.

I assumed she would not be keeping the appointment after all, so we decided to have coffee in the hotel before returning to Ypres. Meeting her after 48 years was a bit too much to ask.

Suddenly, as we drank our coffee, Lucienne appeared in the doorway with her husband Anthony. She recognised me straight away and I her, and she said to Jean 'Leslie has not changed at all'. (Because Ernest is a German sounding name, they called me by my second name Leslie, years ago.) For two hours we talked about old times and Anthony told of his work abroad, in the shipping industry. They were now both retired and had made their home in Antwerp, itself an important shipping city.

I could hardly believe this was really happening and excited conversations between the family took place. After a while Anthony said they must go as they had decorators in at home. We walked with them to near where their car was parked, said our farewells as they left and continued a walk through the streets of the city. Antwerp is a lovely city of marvellous buildings and statues at every corner. We would have liked to explore its narrow streets further but we had to leave for Ypres again.

The meeting with Lucienne and husband Anthony in Antwerp

Back in this First World War frontier town we stopped at the Menin Gate for the 8pm ceremonial playing of the Last Post. I think we all found it very emotional, as we remembered so many thousands of men who had died in its defence long ago. Every evening at 6pm since November 11th 1929 this ceremony has taken place. Later we sat down to a good meal at one of the restaurants that welcome tourists of all nationalities with such warmth and genuine friendliness. It was this same warmth that had endeared me to Ypres and it will forever remain in my memory.

On arrival in Ypres from Antwerp we suddenly remembered that Lucienne and Anthony had told us that they would be celebrating their Ruby Anniversary the coming Saturday. Jean suggested sending them a bouquet from all of us with our good wishes. It was just like her to think of such a nice gesture. The florist was about to close her shop, but we were able to choose some flowers and arrange for them to be sent.

As we stood in the square the next morning ready to leave, the bells of the Cloth Hall belfry chimed out a tune. For me our visit to Normandy and Ypres had been a nostalgic journey back in time and an experience to remember.

Back home in Sittingbourne the following Friday being Good Friday, it seemed appropriate that I should be in the Churches' annual March of Witnesses. I thought of the sacrifices of thousands upon thousands of men and women's lives in two horrible world wars and I thought also of the crucifixion of a carpenter who gave his life 2,000 years ago. Later, on Easter Sunday, I celebrated with many others the victory of that same carpenter who I believe conquered death and who gave a new meaning to life.

Thinking of this tour now, I feel I cannot thank those of my family enough for planning this journey. It is my hope that they too felt something of the emotional effect of those events in our history.

Chapter 11
Reunions

In 1999 I had a surprise telephone call from Margaret who I had got to know during my stay in the seaside town of Bridlington in 1943/44, and had not seen since that time. It brought back many happy memories of my posting there - see Chapter 4. Apparently, Margaret was on her way to the ferry terminal at Ramsgate in Kent for the channel crossing and passing through Gillingham, noticed the name of Sittingbourne on a sign. She had remembered me from my time in Yorkshire, looked my name up in the telephone directory and decided to get in touch. It seemed incredible that after fifty-five years that she could possibly remember me. I could hardly believe that it was her voice after such a long time. So began a series of letters and telephone conversations in which we recalled those far off war time days in Bridlington.

Early in 2000 I received more telephone calls and letters from Margaret, in which she hoped we would be able to visit her in Bridlington sometime during the year. I discovered that she and her husband, David had both served in the forces in Israel during the latter part of the war. Margaret had volunteered and joined the ATS (Auxiliary Territorial Service). David, it seems, loved military history and had read about the exploits of the 11th Armoured Division in Normandy, in which I served. He seemed very interested in reading the potted history of my time in the 23rd Hussars.

Margaret had said on more than one occasion, 'You must come and stay with us in Bridlington soon.' My wife Jean was never altogether happy about the prospect of meeting strangers. I assured her that the people of Yorkshire are very friendly and warm hearted and that she would soon feel very much at ease with them as I had done.

'Let's have a second honeymoon', I suggested. So it was agreed that we would travel to Bridlington and stay for a week with David and Margaret in July. I looked forward to this visit to a town and people who welcomed me so much during the war.

With Margaret in Bridlington 2006

The much planned and talked of journey to Bridlington took place on July 12th. We boarded an express coach from London, having been taken by car by our daughter Jennifer, for the start of the holiday. At Victoria Coach Station we changed coaches for the long journey to Yorkshire. It was very convenient for us that the coach destined for Whitby would be stopping at Bridlington.

It was a pleasant and comfortable journey and as we got nearer our destination Jean became more nervous about meeting people she did not know. She need not have worried. On arrival, at the large and empty coach park, we were met by Margaret and her husband David. While I unloaded our cases, Margaret was already giving Jean a welcome and threw her arms around her saying how pleased she was to meet her at last. For me it was a very happy reunion with Margaret who I had met 55 years before. A few minutes later we arrived at Margaret's house at 30 St James Road and instantly felt at home with them.

So began a week when we talked so much about our experiences. A great deal of the conversations were about David's time in the Colonial Service for the police and we found he and Margaret had lived a very interesting life. Also, it was good for me too to recall those days in 1943/44. David took us for a tour of the old town where at St John's Methodist Church I had found such a warm welcome as a soldier and met Margaret. One morning we drove to the Moors I knew so well, visiting the pretty villages of Thornton-le-Dale and Hutton-le-Hole. Eventually we arrived at Whitby where we all enjoyed a fish and chip lunch at a popular restaurant. On another occasion, we travelled to Flamborough Head and at Bempton Cliffs we watched the hundreds of seabirds. Cormorants, puffins and many other seabirds could be seen perched precariously on the narrow ledges of the cliff face. It is said that 20,000 birds visit this area.

During the week we visited the new Anglican Emmanuel Church, which had only been opened about a year before and the church Margaret attends occasionally.

Sunday morning found us at the service at the Quay Methodist Church which I had attended many years previously. After the service we had coffee in the hall behind the church and I remembered that in this hall a concert was arranged for the servicemen on Sunday evenings long ago. The memories came flooding back to those days before the regiment left to travel south for preparations for the Normandy landings (not that we knew this until a few days before the crossing).

As we wanted to take some kind of souvenir of our visit, we had asked my son-in-law Keith to engrave a bowl for us with appropriate illustrations of Kent. The result was a beautiful crystal bowl as a reminder of the ship building trades of Sittingbourne and etchings of hops, cherries and apples. The words beautifully traced in the glass, 'Flavours of Kent July 1999' completed the design. Margaret and David were noticeably thrilled with the gift and David said he would pass it on to Amy, one of his grandchildren.

The week in Bridlington was a complete success and Margaret said before we boarded our coach to come home, 'Promise me you will come again next year'.

Our second pilgrimage to Bridlington began on July 10th 2012. We were warmly welcomed again to Margaret's home, not far from the Spa Leisure Centre and South Promenade. This time we were to spend two or three pleasant afternoons on the beach because of the warmer weather, even daring to enter the sea. It was not really warm enough to swim however.

Margaret took me to the Priory Church where, to my surprise and amazement there is a memorial to those of the 23rd Hussars, C Squadron who died during the first six months of the war in 1944. Of the four squadrons of the 23rd Hussars, I was pleased to see that my squadron had been remembered. The names of my Troop Commander, Lt Peter Robson, and Troop Sergeant, Sgt McIntosh, with others I had known were embossed in gold on a specially carved memorial. The flag of the regiment stood next to it and David took my photograph, with me wearing my beret with the 23rd

H badge on it. It seemed as if Bridlington had adopted the regiment, such a place of honour was it given.

C Squadron 23rd Hussars Memorial in Priory Church Bridlington

An afternoon trip out to Flamborough was made more interesting because of a helicopter which appeared to be doing some exercise flying near cliffs. I imagine it was often called upon to rescue climbers in difficulty. We took the moorland train from Pickering to Goathland, TV's Heartbeat country, crossing the wild countryside in which I had trained back in 1943/44.

We went to church in the Methodist Chapel, in the old part of the town again, and attended the little prayer group who met at the Emmanuel Church, just a street away from David and Margaret's home. They were a very friendly group and we talked afterwards over a cup of coffee. After two weeks in the Yorkshire resort we took the coach for our journey home. The visit once again brought back to me happy memories of my stay there before leaving for Normandy in 1944.

Two very interesting things I almost forgot to mention. Margaret sent me a letter which she had received while in the forces. It was from the Reverend Douglas Morallee, who had been the minister of St John's Church in Bridlington before she joined the ATS. Apparently, and I did not know this, Bill Morallee followed his brother Douglas when he finished his ministry in the August of 1944. Many years later I told Margaret that William Morallee came to Sittingbourne as our second minister and shared the marriage ceremony at Newington of our daughter Jennifer and Keith, with a previous man, who Jean and I became close friends with, Reverend Bill Prince.

Another amazing coincidence I discovered was that Bridlington is twinned with Bad Salzuflen where I was stationed in 1945/46. Banners with the coat of arms of the German Spa town were even displayed in the shopping precinct.

In 2006 an unexpected message received on our church web site caused some interest regarding my old regiment, the 23rd Hussars. It appeared that an ex-member of the regiment, of B Squadron had seen an article that I had written in the Bridlington Methodist magazine. This had prompted him to get in touch with Tony Brown of our local Wesley Methodist Church in Sittingbourne, via a message to the church web site. The person, Bill Gray assumed that I was a Methodist minister and wanted to find out more about me. He mentioned that for a number of years there had been annual reunions of the 23rd Hussars in Bridlington on Remembrance Day. Although the official reunions had ceased the previous year, a small group intended to keep the meetings going. He hoped that I would be able to attend the annual Remembrance Day service to be held at the Priory Church in Bridlington in November. This became a topic of conversation in the family, the result being that I was to go to this reunion. I intended travelling up to Bridlington by National Express coach as Jean and I had done to stay with Margaret and David Cook. However, my children, David and Jennifer offered to take me by car. This was decided and I was very much looking forward to the service and meeting some men of the squadron.

We had a good journey to Yorkshire, arriving in the town at 4.30pm. My wife Jean was not well and could not come with me, so we called to see how she was. My granddaughter Rebecca was keeping an eye on her at home, in case she needed help (Jean had insisted that I should go as it was only for a weekend).

We were welcomed to 30 St James Road by Margaret who had cooked us an evening meal, after which we settled into our rooms. To be back in Bridlington again was good for me, although the weather was very cold, but fortunately dry and sunny. That evening we went with Margaret to the Ravensbrook Hotel where about ten members of my old regiment were due to meet. They had been meeting in Bridlington for a number of years, on Remembrance Day. I met Bill Gray, from 'B' Squadron. We talked for some time and then another beckoned to me. He was the only one from my 'C' squadron, who had been able to come. His name was Michael Binney from Durham and we had a very interesting conversation over drinks. He remembered Peter Robson, our troop commander, and also Sgt McIntosh who was killed in Caen during Operation Goodwood. In fact, he said he and another man helped him (Sgt McIntosh) from the turret of his tank and buried him after a shell had skimmed the top of the tank, severing his head in the process. It must have been a gruesome task having to do this and lay his body to rest. I had heard about this but I never believed it really happened, until then.

The following day, Remembrance Day, we went to Priory Church and met the same men who we had met the previous evening.

Bill Gray 23rd Hussars, with his wife at Priory Church

It was good to be with veterans from my regiment again on that day, so many years after our war time training in the area.

It was a beautiful service and I was particularly interested in listening to the robed choir and the organ. The Priory Church in Bridlington is an imposing building and the music set the scene for the occasion. In the front row I heard Bill whisper something to Michael who was sitting next to him. However, I did catch part of the conversation. He said 'He is laying the wreath. He doesn't know about it yet'.

At the appropriate time Bill handed me the wreath and with him and Michael as escorts I followed the procession to the west door, behind the vicar and the bugler. It was a very emotional moment for me, as I thought of all those of the 23rd Hussars I had known, and who did not come home. I thought of the many battles we had been involved in. At the regimental memorial I laid the wreath and had a brief look at the names I knew so well, carved into the memorial panels. I was pleased that I was able to perform this ceremony.

After the service we wandered along the seafront's South Promenade and visited the town. Where the Quay Methodist Church once stood, was a new shopping centre. I thought of all the times I had worshipped there in 1944.

On the front the Spa Royal Hall and Theatre was undergoing a major refurbishment. The engineers had encountered a water source beneath the foundations which would need a great deal of extra attention. These were actually springs. This set back the opening date by many months and it would not be ready for the summer of 2007, as planned.

On Monday we said our farewells and began the journey home. It had been a good weekend meeting old friends and making new ones.

In 2005, the BBC invited people to enter their war experiences on a website entitled 'WW2 People's War', as an archive of WW2 memories. My granddaughter Rebecca had edited a section of the second edition of my autobiography and loaded it onto the web site. During the latter part of August 2012, I received a letter from Mr Frank Grimshaw of Preston. He had seen my article on the BBC website. He had also been in the 23rd Hussars and he sent me some photographs of C Squadron entering Antwerp in September 1944. We kept in touch for a while and he said he hoped to be in Bridlington in November. However, on ringing him one afternoon his wife informed me that he had been taken into hospital with a suspected blood clot and he was very ill. Later his son Neil wrote to me to say that he would be going to the service in his father's place and hoped to meet me. Tragically his father died suddenly a few days later. Although I had never met him, I felt a connection in some way.

Priory Church Bridlington

Priory Church Bridlington

In the July of 2012, Stan, a friend of Margaret's, had suggested to me that he thought it would be appropriate for me, being a local preacher and ex-member of the 23rd Hussars, to give a short address during the Remembrance service at the Bridlington Priory Church on November 11th. I hardly imagined the vicar would agree to this, but Stan said he intended to ask if this was possible.

A week before I was due to travel with my family to Yorkshire, he rang me to tell me that all had been arranged with the curate (the vicar had moved on to another church). I was surprised about this but set about composing something that would be suitable for the occasion.

Together with my two children Jennifer and David, and David's wife Carole we travelled to Yorkshire and booked into a guest house.

On Remembrance Day we attended the service at Priory Church and I was asked to say the Eulogy after the playing of the Last Post. The service went well and in addition to Jennifer, David and Carole, was attended by Margaret, her daughter Jane and husband Robin, plus Carole's mother and sister Pat, who came down from Middlesbrough. The 23rd Hussars was represented, as usual by a group of surviving members of the regiment, of which there were only four that year. Also, I was very pleased to meet Fred Grimshaw's son Neil again, before we entered the church.

There was a fully robed choir, with small boys dressed in scarlet robes, who sang so well in the anthems and hymns. My Eulogy seemed to go well, and it was a very enjoyable weekend for all of us.

As is quite evident in this book I feel quite at home in any church, especially the Anglican Communion with its liturgy and love of ceremony.

Chapter 12
Return to Holland and Germany

Early in 2012 I happened to mention to my children Jennifer and David that I would like one day to return to Germany. This started David looking to book a flight to Hannover and hiring a car at the airport. The plan was to spend two days in Bad Salzuflen and two days in Fallingbostel. I had stayed at both towns in 1945/46 as recounted in Chapter 7.

In Bad Salzuflen I had hoped to be able to stay at the Quellenhof where I lived in 1945 but discovered this was now a steakhouse. Happily enough we were to reserve rooms at the Rosengarten Hotel, which happened to be directly opposite the Quellenhof.

In due course all was arranged. In the party would be me, my son David with his wife Carole and their children Helen and Philip, both in their twenties together with my daughter Jennifer. I was very much looking forward to the trip, and eager to show the family around the places in Germany that I remembered so well.

On Saturday May 5th we set out for our few days in Germany. We flew to Hannover where we hired an eight-seater vehicle and set off for Bad Salzuflen. We arrived in the town at about lunch time and booked into the Rosengarten Hotel, situated at the entrance to the Kirkpark. Opposite was the Quellenhof, where I had many happy months all those years ago. After settling into our rooms, we took our first tour of the town. It happened that there was a festival that weekend and there were many stalls along the streets. There was a drum band beating out music and quite a crowd in the streets. The buildings, half-timbered and intricately decorated facades were so attractive, many of five and six stories tall, with tiny windows in the roofs. It was just as I remembered it, although now there were more people about. Everywhere there was an atmosphere of happy social life. Like most continental towns Bad Salzuflen had attractive squares where people gathered. Such places bring people together to meet and enjoy themselves. We could learn a lot from these towns I thought. In comparison our towns are sometimes unattractive and merely shopping centres. There they are so much better. The stalls were full of attractive gifts, food and clothes. In the evenings these stalls were decorated with coloured lights, which made it magical. During our brief stay we spent time exploring Kirkpark with its tulip filled flower beds and neat lawns. There was a large lake at the end of the park where boats could be hired. A modern tourist information building and concert hall has been built in the park since the war.

The Quellenhof Hotel where I was based in 1945,
with my son and grandson

Bad Salzuflen sits on a source of underground salt water which is pumped into tall T shaped structures. These 'graduation houses' as they are called are large wooden frames filled with bunches of blackthorn. The salt water or brine is pumped to the top and passes through the blackthorn giving off a fine spray of vitalising vapours, good for treating many ailments. Between these 'hedges' for want

Headquarters of GHQ Troops, Bad Salzuflen

Kirkpark, Bad Salzuflen

of a better word, people may sit in the soft glow of lamps and the sound of music to take in the health-giving minerals.

Also, there are buildings in the park with baths where people can take the health-giving waters. One can climb to the top of these graduation towers for a view of the town. After eight months of construction in 2007 these houses and facilities were reconstructed and a truly unique feature of the town, extracting the brine from depths of 50 – 100 metres to be passed through the graduation houses. I felt that I could happily spend a month here, not only enjoying the spa but also the surrounding countryside.

I discovered the building just inside the entrance to the park, which was the headquarters of GHQ troops, where I had worked. It had changed little though over the years. How Jean, my wife would have loved to have visited this picturesque part of Germany I thought.

On the third day of our tour we set off for the town of Fallingbostel where I had completed my army service. This town lies north of Hannover.

We arrived at Fallingbostel in the early afternoon and checked into a hotel just outside the town which was accessible to places we intended to visit. I realised how much the town had grown since I was there in 1946. It was then just a small village about a mile from our camp, the No 3 Civilian Internment Camp[13] (CIC). I tried to find the TOC H building as it had been when I was there, but was unable to do so initially. Before we left, however, we found a building marked on the map as Martin Luther House. I felt quite sure that this must be the place I had been looking for.

---

[13] The CIC was for German professionals who were suspected of collaborating with the Nazi regime.

We made enquiries about the camp that I was in and were put in touch with someone who had responsibility for the area at a place called Oerbke. I was sure that our unit must have been somewhere here in the countryside north of Fallingbostel centre. This area had become a NATO training ground, and at the time of our visit there was still a British 7th Armoured Division stationed there. The camp commissioner at Oerbke invited us to his centre and told us a lot about the camps that the German military had set up as prisoner of war camps. He showed us a map in which there were such camps which once housed Russian and Polish prisoners. The camp names were Stalag X1A and X1B. Stalag X1C was in fact Belson concentration camp about 6 miles away.

The camp where I was based in 1945/46, No 3 CIC was converted from a German prisoner of war camp, to a prison for German civilians, after cessation of hostilities. It is likely to have been one of the Stalag camps but which one could not be confirmed. I remembered that when I was there, it consisted of wooden huts like a prison camp. It was probably somewhere in this area but I did not find it, and much of the area had now become woodland. There were concrete foundations in the woods but nothing to confirm where No 3 CIC had actually been located. Perhaps with more time we could have researched further and found it.

Not far away was the town of Munster with a military museum. On display were a large number of German armoured vehicles which included the once dreaded Tiger 88mm tank. I was also interested to find a Sherman 17-pounder, still bearing the badge of the Black Bull of the 11th Armoured Division and the new British Comet which the regiment advanced into Germany with in 1945.

A much more pleasant site we visited was Vogel Park Gardens. They were celebrating the 50th anniversary of its opening. It was a large park of brilliant tulip filled gardens with areas for wildlife. Several little lakes and ponds housed pelicans, penguins and flamingos in natural surroundings. Feeding time attracted large numbers of visitors. Also, in large cages, a variety of parrots and other wild birds with a riot of brilliant plumage perched on branches. After the solemn atmosphere of the tank museum, this was a pleasant way to spend the afternoon.

The next day being the last day of our brief visit to Germany we decided to visit Belson Concentration Camp. I learned some time after the war, that it was my regiment, the 23rd Hussars who had come across the camp in the advance northwards. We arrived to see large gaunt concrete buildings which housed many artefacts. We entered the exhibition through tall black steel doors. The events of the life of this place are portrayed in sequence. There are letters and photographs documenting the days up to its discovery. It relates in detail the capture, imprisonment and cruel murder of thousands of men women and children, most of them Jews. It tells of slave labour and indescribable violent treatment of the inmates. Special mention is made of the young woman, Anne Frank who hid from the Gestapo for many months in Holland. There was a small cinema showing ghastly scenes of prisoners' naked bodies being thrown into long deep graves from lorries. I took one very brief look at the horrible scenes and could not stay a moment longer. I have to say that I unashamedly cried at the thought of this inhumane treatment of innocent people.

The story continues on the second floor and there are photographs of the guards, some young women, who were on the staff, and their eventual prosecution. Later, in pouring rain, we walked around the large cemetery where mounds of earth now covered in grass marked the graves of hundreds of victims. Engraved stones on each mound indicated the number buried beneath, marked 5,000 here, 8,000 there, and there were memorials to the thousands of Jews; the race that the Nazis were bent on exterminating. It was terrifying to see what lengths Hitler and the Gestapo had taken to inflict such suffering. The memory of this place will stay with me for ever. One hopes that such things will never happen again.

In winter 1941/42, the German advances in the Soviet Union came to a halt. The Wehrmacht drafted more and more soldiers and thus required more and more arms and ammunition. This situation led to a massive labour shortage within the German war economy and forced the German government to fundamentally reconsider its policy towards the Soviet POWs. They were now considered indispensable workers who had to be fed and treated better.

From the summer of 1942, most Soviet POWs were deployed to work details and satellite camps. The Oerbke and Wietzendorf camps became branch camps of Stalag XI B at Fallingbostel and X B at Sandbostel, while camp XI C (311) at Bergen-Belsen remained in operation until the spring of 1943. Then the SS took over one half of the camp and set up a concentration camp there.

The Wehrmacht continued to operate the POW field hospital, but reclassified it as the "Bergen-Belsen branch camp" of Stalag XI B in Fallingbostel. Soviet POWs and, from 1944, Italian military internees were treated at the hospital.

In October 1944, Polish soldiers and officers who had taken part in the Warsaw Uprising were also incarcerated in the Bergen-Belsen branch camp.

Detail from the museum at Belson Concentration Camp, referring to Fallingbostel

Belson Concentration Camp

Belson Concentration Camp

Holland

In 2018 my son David arranged a trip to Holland to visit several places where I spent time during the war. This was another country I wanted to re-visit, remembering those wet and miserable weeks in 1944, holding the line near the River Maas where we had been shelled, testing our nerves.

Leunen, the village where my regiment was positioned, was very quiet the morning we arrived and I immediately recognised the church and primary school now renovated, where children were on their break and noisily playing outside. There were a few local people out and about and I spoke to one elderly couple who remembered the British troops in the village, indicating that one soldier was buried there, but I believe subsequently moved. Leunen was now a small town with many new houses. It was very peaceful and pleasant compared to my time there in 1944 during a winter when it rained incessantly and shelling tortured our nerves.

Leunen with son-in-law Keith and daughter-in-law Carole

We went on to visit Arnhem where so many men lost their lives in 1944, as they parachuted into the north of the city to hold the bridge, which of course they failed to do. At that time my regiment was travelling up to support them but did not arrive in time to avoid a significant defeat for the Allies. We visited the cemetery where many of the parachutists were buried between swathes of neatly trimmed grass. I well remember in 1944 looking up as the regiment travelled north, to the hundreds of gliders transporting paratroopers to their landing zone.

Cemetery near Arnhem, many Polish and other paratroopers killed in the failed attack to take Arnhem Bridge

The people of this part of Holland suffered a great deal at that time and it was moving to see a fiftieth anniversary tribute to the Dutch people and the Resistance by the British and Polish Airborne Forces.

A tribute to the Dutch People near Arnhem

Inscription on the stone:

'50 years ago British and Polish Airborne soldiers fought here against overwhelming odds to open the way into Germany and bring the war to an early end. Instead we brought death and destruction for which you have never blamed us.

This stone marks our admiration for your great courage remembering especially the women who tended our wounded. In the long winter that followed your families risked death by hiding Allied soldiers and airmen while members of the Resistance helped many to safety.

You took us into your homes as fugitives and friends, we took you into our hearts. This strong bond will continue long after we are gone.'

1944 - September-1994

Chapter 13
Legion of Honour

During a trip to Bridlington in 2015 I met Bill Gray of the 23rd Hussars and he told me that President Francois Hollande of France had decided to award the French Legion of Honour medal to those who fought to liberate France. The Legion of Honour (French: Légion d'honneur) is the highest French order of merit for military and civilians, established in 1802 by Napoleon Bonaparte.

Presented with the Legion of Honour by the French Consul

I received the medal some weeks later and it was arranged that it would be formally presented with eight other veterans by the French Consul at Dover College. There was no limitation on family members invited to join me at the presentation, so on January 17th I was joined by 14 members of the family. Each veteran was cited individually during a wonderful service led by the Chaplain with a robed choir. An opportunity to talk to other veterans followed in the adjacent refectory. I felt very honoured to receive such a high award being just one of thousands who experienced those months in Normandy in 1944. Many of my compatriots had passed on and did not live long enough to receive this medal, I felt proud and very humble. It is not every day that one receives such gratitude for one's achievements. I was one of those lucky enough to come out of the conflict physically unscathed.

**Outside Dover College after the ceremony (top),
and being interviewed by the BBC (bottom)**

Chatting with another veteran at Dover College

With the whole family who accompanied me to the ceremony

Chapter 14
Bovington Tank Museum

In 2016 I was approached by the local Heritage Society in Sittingbourne to ask if I would be willing to man a stall at a planned 'Armed Forces Day' in the town centre, and speak to people about my experiences, as a Second World War Normandy veteran. Perhaps they were aware that I, like all other second world war Normandy veterans, had been awarded The Legion of Honour medal by the French President earlier that year and had managed to find my address. At the event I displayed many photographs which I had acquired over the years and was able to meet and talk to many people. Being the guest of honour, I really felt important!

Later that year my son David planned a visit to Bovington Tank Museum in Dorset. He had been in touch with the museum and they were keen to have a Second World War veteran radio operator from a Sherman Tank visit. The museum houses a Sherman Firefly Tank, the model that I was in, and the idea was that I should be positioned next to the tank and talk to visitors about my experiences. In addition, the museum was filming interviews from tank crew veterans, to be shown in their refurbished Second World War hall, and I was invited to participate. I travelled to the museum with my son and daughter in law and spent a few days in this lovely part of Dorset.

On the first morning of my visit I was filmed being interviewed about my experiences during the war. In the afternoon they set me up next to the Sherman Firefly Tank in their exhibition hall, together with a number of enlarged photographs from that time which I had brought with me. I spent the afternoon chatting to visitors about my wartime experiences in the tank.

With the Sherman Firefly at Bovington

This proved to be very popular and I frequently had a queue of people waiting to speak to me. This was an enjoyable experience and lots of people wished to have their photos taken with me next to this enormous tank. I repeated this for a few hours the following day before touring the local area and returning home to Kent.

Talking to visitors next to the Sherman Firefly

Talking to children at Bovington

Early in 2017 I was invited to visit the museum once again. They were holding an opening ceremony for a new special exhibition of Tiger Tanks in the April of that year. As part of the ceremony they had invited two British and two German tank crew veterans to meet. I attended together with Dr Ken Tout, a veteran from the Northampton Yeomanry Regiment. It was an honour to be invited to meet the 'enemy' so to speak, face to face. It was something I never expected to happen, especially after so many years. I looked forward to this event and was driven down to Dorset by my son David and his wife Carole, staying overnight nearby the night before.

The opening ceremony was a quite significant affair for the museum who had invited a number of reporters and senior armed service personnel. It started with pre-ceremony drinks in the large new exhibition hall, where several massive Tiger tanks had been positioned. On one wall was a video display of several tank crew speaking of their time in the war, and my interview filmed some months previously was included. I chatted with Dr Ken Tout the other British tank man and then the two German tank crew members arrived. We shook hands and greeted each other with the help of an interpreter. The four of us sat side by side in front of one of the Tiger tanks for a photo opportunity from a battery of reporters and camera men. I had never been photographed so much in my life. We were treated as VIPs. However, we were simply four men still alive from the battles of 1944. There were very few of us left.

Chatting with David Willey, Museum Curator and Dr Ken Tout, 1st Northants Yeomanry, before the Tiger Exhibition opening ceremony

Among the Tiger tank collection was one known as The Elephant. It was enormous and weighed about 65 tonnes, brought over from a museum in America on loan to Bovington. We never saw these monster machines close up during the war. The 88mm gun of The King Tiger tank could fire from as far away as 2 kilometres and knock out a Sherman Tank, which often turned into a ball of fire (hence the term 'Tommy cookers').

From the Left, Waldemar Pliska, Ernie Slarks, Wilhelm Fischer and Ken Tout at Bovington Tank Museum

The Sherman Firefly with its 17lb gun in which I served as radio operator/loader could destroy a Tiger, so long as the Sherman attacked broadside on. It was much lighter than the Tiger but had the advantage of being faster and more manoeuvrable.

After meeting and chatting with the German tank crew we went off individually to speak to waiting reporters from newspapers, radio and TV. Following the official opening by David Willey, the museum curator and other dignitaries and press interviews, we had lunch together with the German crewmen and their families, ending a very memorable day.

In 2019 the museum contacted me to say that they had built a scale model of a Sherman tank for children's educational purposes. They proposed to call it 'Ernie the Sherman'. I was honoured to have a model tank named after me and travelled down to the museum to see it. The model was very impressive. It was very well made (of plastic and wood I believe) and was accurate to scale. It could be assembled by 7-12 year old children under the supervision of Claire, the museum's Education Officer, and whilst I was there, she explained all about the tank to a large group of children crowded round. As in the previous year I was able to spend some time sitting next to the full-size Sherman in the Tank Hall, and chatting to museum visitors.

With Ernie the Sherman at Bovington Tank Museum

Chapter 15
D-Day 75th Anniversary Voyage

Early in 2019 my son-in-law Keith mentioned that the British Legion were planning a 'Voyage of Remembrance' for veterans of the WW2 Normandy Campaign, to coincide with the 75th anniversary of D-Day, to acknowledge the service of all those who served and survived, and for those who gave their lives in this critical invasion to push back and defeat the Germans. My son David applied for me to go and I was subsequently accepted, together with about 250 other veterans each accompanied by carers. (David came as my carer). The Voyage of Remembrance was a six-day cruise on the Fred Olsen Cruise Liner, MV Boudicca.

MV Boudicca

The cruise started in Dover where we embarked MV Boudicca accompanied by music from a local band, and an escort of local scouts. Over the following days we were to travel to Dunkirk, Poole, Portsmouth and Le Havre near the Normandy landing sites.

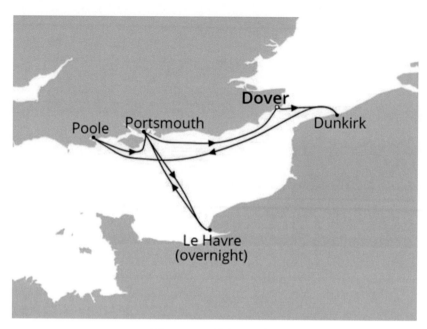

The route of the cruise

The first afternoon was spent on board in Dover where the Royal British Legion Military Band played music on the rear deck, and Rod Stewart made a special appearance and met many veterans. There were many reporters on board, all keen to hear stories from the veterans and my first interview was with ITN on that first afternoon.

We were addressed by the President of the Royal British Legion at an introductory talk that first evening when he said 'This is a Voyage of Remembrance of all those who gave their lives in WW2, but it is also for all of you here, the last of the veterans who are still alive. All this is for you chaps. Enjoy it. My British Legion staff are here to provide every support so please don't hesitate to ask.'

Royal British Legion Central Band playing on deck

On that first evening we departed Dover, accompanied by tugs offering a salute with massive jets of water, as the band played military tunes.

The next morning, Monday 3rd June we had arrived in Dunkirk. Dunkirk was chosen as the first stop as a fitting low point in WW2, and we moored in a remote part of the harbour far from the busy port area. Some of the veterans on board were evacuated from here in 1940 following the rapid advance of German troops through France towards the coast. It was a quiet day of reflection and getting to know other veterans. We were warned that we had busy days ahead and to take advantage of this break before the extensive travelling and ceremonies of the following days.

Overnight on Monday we travelled back across the Channel to Poole. We were given a wonderful welcome by the Marine Commandos at the harbour in Poole. They had brought modern military equipment for us to examine, and more reporters were there. I was interviewed by a Dutch radio reporter.

Group photo of all the veterans, as we moored at Dunkirk

Also, there was a large group of children from the local primary school who were all keen to meet the veterans, and obviously had been primed not to be nervous but come and say hello. In the evening we left Poole for the short overnight journey to Portsmouth.

Talking to school children in Poole Harbour

The following day, Wednesday 5th June was to be the main commemoration ceremony in the UK, and was held at Southsea Common in Portsmouth. We disembarked into about 12 coaches to take all veterans and carers from the port to the event. Disembarking so many veterans, some of whom were in wheelchairs, was a lengthy process. Owing to the steep slope of the ramp to shore, all veterans were required to sit in wheelchairs and be pushed by soldiers on hand to assist. Our coaches travelled the few miles to Southsea Common through heavy security. Roads had been closed to secure our route, and that of the Queen and many world leaders attending the ceremony.

Amongst the several world leaders to speak, President Trump introduced a recording of Eisenhower's D-Day message to the Allied Forces '…You are about to embark on a great crusade….. the hopes and prayers of liberty loving people everywhere march with you'

With my son David before the ceremony at Portsmouth

After the ceremony, in the veterans' marquee, I spoke to Theresa May our outgoing Prime Minister, and Mr Macron the President of France. World leaders were all keen to speak to the veterans.

It was wonderful that our Queen sat amongst us in the Veterans' stand with leaders of America, Canada and Europe to share the occasion. During the ceremony, a frigate passed by in the estuary nearby giving a horn salute and the Red Arrows roared overhead, flying in formation across the seated servicemen in front of the stage.

With Theresa May

With President Macron

At the end of the event our twelve coaches slowly made their way back to the boat through streets lined with police and many local well-wishers.

In early evening we dropped our moorings and headed out from Portsmouth on our journey to the Normandy beaches. We were accompanied by two frigates, one British and one Canadian, together with other naval craft. As we passed out of the harbour, hundreds of people had congregated to see us off. On a small beach area, a simple but moving gesture had been erected – the words 'Thank you' in ten-foot-high white lettering.

**At the stern of MV Boudicca leaving Portsmouth
escorted by British and Canadian Frigates**

As we sailed out of the estuary, we passed the massive new aircraft carrier, Queen Elizabeth. The entire length of the deck was lined with sailors in perfect formation, offering a salute. A number of other naval ships paraded past us coming into port, sailors lining the decks. Three cheers were called from a passing frigate and we could clearly see the white naval caps raised in salute.

Further out into the estuary, as we stood on the aft deck, a lone Spitfire approached from the stern against the setting sun and flew low over the ship with that unmistakable roar of the Merlin engine – a very moving moment, captured by my son on video.

Queen Elizabeth Aircraft Carrier with full crew saluting the veterans

Frigate saluting the veterans as it passed MV Boudicca

At sunset, just off Ventnor on the Isle of Wight, MV Boudicca paused before the crossing to France, for an address on deck by the President of the Royal British Legion to honour the men who gathered there. I quote from his speech '...in these very waters, on this very evening 75 years ago was assembling the largest maritime assault force the world had ever known'. This was a poignant tribute before we made the same journey.

President of the Royal British Legion speaking at sunset off the Isle of Wight

We moored in Le Havre the following morning and disembarked for the journey to Bayeux War Cemetery, 78 miles to the west. Much of the route had been closed for us and French troops and police could be seen at all junctions and overbridges. We arrived shortly before Charles and Camilla who arrived in their entourage and were whisked away to a special marquee.

The cemetery is beautifully kept and was a fitting location for a commemorative service in front of the main memorial cross. I laid a wreath after the service, in memory of the men I knew, and after the ceremony found over a dozen graves of the men in my regiment, the 23rd Hussars. During the service I was able to sing well known hymns accompanied by a French military band and the choir from Hereford Cathedral. I was interviewed by French TV and also got chatting to a Spanish photographer, and a local man from Arromanches.

Ceremony at Bayeux War Cemetery

Graves of 23rd Hussars, Bayeux War Cemetery

With Prince Charles

In the veteran's marquee after the main ceremony, I met Prince Charles and Camilla, I had a long chat with Prince Charles who commented 'it must have been awful in a tank'.

The Royal British Legion Central Band played in the marquee and Land of Hope and Glory was played with six encores, with soloist Emma Brown!

After another tiring day we headed back to the ship to be entertained by evening shows and the Royal British Legion Central Band.

The next day, Friday 7th June we travelled to the landing beaches. My particular coach travelled to Arromanches where we were marched into the village, escorted by British troops and a French military band. Local people lined our route and the welcome was overwhelming. Many local people wished to shake my hand and thank me for being part of the Normandy Invasion, which freed France in the course of the war. The Mayor of Arromanches gave each veteran €100 to spend whilst we were there.

With French School Children in Arromanches

Shaking Hands with local French woman at Arromanches

After the main visit to Arromanches our coach stopped at two other landing beaches and I planted a cross on Sword Beach in memory of those who fell in the early days of the invasion.

Planting a cross on Sword Beach with another veteran

Sword Beach

Back on board the MV Boudicca that evening there was a special show for the veterans, with music from the 40s including the 'D-Day Darlings', a trio of girls dressed in forces uniforms.

We were due to return to Portsmouth the following day (Saturday 8th) before going on to Dover to disembark. However the weather was very windy and the captain decided we should head straight for Dover. It was nice to see a small group of well-wishers on the dockside as we entered Dover, who had obviously found out we would be there early and come out to welcome us home.

As we boarded our coach for the journey back home, the President of the Royal British Legion came on to wish us a safe journey and to invite us to contact the organisation if we needed help or support at any time in the future.

This cruise was a wonderful experience and I am very grateful for the Royal British Legion and the staff of MV Boudicca. The staff and volunteers on board were absolutely amazing in their empathy and care for some very frail veterans. Nothing was too much trouble and all events were designed to honour us as veterans.

With my son David on MV Boudicca

Postscript

I hope this story of my experiences over nearly a century, starting in the 1920s, has provided some insight into the life of an ordinary man from Kent whose life has spanned some troubled times.

How can I finish?

It is normal for a father to give some advice to his children as they grow up. Now that I have grandchildren and great grandchildren perhaps they may also be interested in my thoughts. So for them all, I end with these words of an anonymous writer which I came across many years ago. They seem to me to be very wise and have remained with me ever since.

" I shall pass through this world but once.

Any kind word that I can utter, or any good thing that I can do, let me do it NOW.

Let me not forget it, or defer it, for I shall not pass this way again".

Ernest Slarks, Sittingbourne, Kent
March 2020

Index